Patrick Pennell
gift from
Clare and Jared Edwards
Christmas, 2019

HOUSE NUMBERS

Published by Reaktion Books Ltd
Unit 32, Waterside
44–48 Wharf Road
London N1 7UX, UK
www.reaktionbooks.co.uk


First published in English by Reaktion Books 2015
© Reaktion Books 2015

Translated by Anthony Mathews

Printed and bound in China by Toppan Printing Co. Ltd

A catalogue record for this book is available from the British Library

ISBN 978 1 78023 518 9

# HOUSE NUMBERS
## Pictures of a Forgotten History

Anton Tantner

REAKTION BOOKS

## A Footnote to History

This short book is about something that is thought to be a footnote to history: the house number. This device has become so commonplace that it never even occurs to people that it could have a history. But just like many other commonplace things which seem always to have existed, the everyday house number was once upon a time an invention, something that had to be introduced into people's day-to-day lives. This was by no means a simple process, meeting as it did with a lot of opposition and difficulty.

The house number saw its greatest moment of triumph in the period of absolutism, in what is called the Age of Enlightenment. It wasn't introduced so that people living and working in towns and villages could find their way around more easily. Nor was it intended to be particularly helpful to travellers. Instead, it started life in that grey area between the military, the tax authorities and early modern policing. It arose out of the 'dust of events', as Foucault calls it, that until recently has rarely appeared in history books.[1]

Numbering houses is a way of designating an address. A house number allocates each house its own unique position and enables the state to know all about the citizens who live there. In this way, during the development of the state in early modern times, a house was officially distinguished from those around it. For those living in the house and their neighbours, the walls simply surrounded an 'open house'.[2] For the purposes of the state, on the other hand, they were obstacles that got in the way. So long as there was no official system of designating an address, the house stood like a monolith that concealed its wealth and belongings within itself. This made it difficult for the tax and military authorities, which lacked precise local knowledge, to keep tabs on them.

## House Names and House Numbers

The meagre evidence relating to house addresses in ancient times suggests that, where they existed, they were based on the owner's name.[3] In Roman towns the inscriptions on slaves' collars indicating where a possible runaway slave was to be returned to sometimes gave the name of a building. But often the owner's name and a rough indication of the area in the city of Rome were sufficient for the return of the slave to the right address.[4] Until the late medieval period there was no great need to give the exact address of a house. In societies where most relations were based on personal acquaintanceship, a person's name and the approximate indication of a place were all that was thought necessary to find them. In Marseille as late as the fourteenth century, creditors noted down only the rudimentary addresses – for example, the street names – of those who owed them debts, that being all that was required to get hold of them if need be.[5]

Before the introduction of house numbers the name of a house, which was often different to that of the owner, was the usual way of identifying it.[6] However, with the growth of central control on the part of the authorities and the associated requirement of state officials to know all about the belongings within individual houses, the disadvantages of addresses based on the names of houses became apparent. The name was after all not always visible, since not every house displayed a sign.

Detail of a wall tablet indicating the profession of the occupier, Amsterdam, Netherlands. Stone plaques such as this were used before house numbers were added.

Knowledge of an address in a locality was limited to the neighbourhood and the local lord. State officials were therefore dependent on local knowledge. They had to rely on the aid of the local lord's officials, whose interests were likely to be conflicted.

But even when house names were visible and listed on a register, addresses based on them were problematic. There was a limit to people's inventiveness at naming houses. The result was a lot of similar-sounding house names that could be confused. In Vienna at the end of the eighteenth century there were six houses in the city centre with the name The Golden Eagle, and a further 23 in the suburbs. In other words, there were 29 houses that could be confused with one another if the house name alone was given.[7] In addition, house names were not fixed but altered with each change of ownership; the renaming

of a house was a display of power and a symbol of
occupation by new owners.[8]

A house number issued by the state, on the other
hand, had the advantage of creating discrete, clearly
distinguishable and fixed units. Once a sign was nailed
on the wall of a house or painted on and left to dry,
it was linked as ineradicably as possible to the house.
It enabled recruiting officers, tax collectors and court
officials to know what was inside. In effect, it made the
walls transparent.

## The 'Whole House' and the House Number

From the socio-historical point of view, the numbering
of houses has been seen as taking place in tandem with
the disappearance of the 'whole house'. The replacement
of house names with abstract numbers was thus an
expression of the idea that the house was to be seen as
separate from the people living in it.[9] The house number
was to bring an end to this 'whole house' and summon in
the age of the family as a new socio-historical entity. This
point of view relates to the debate around the term 'the
whole house', which was made current by Otto Brunner.[10]
What is being described here, however, needs some
clarification. The sequence of events may even have
to be reversed. You could argue that the numbering of
houses should be seen as a precondition for the discourse
around the 'whole house' in the nineteenth century. This
is the influential myth that presents a narrative of a social
process that started in the Neolithic and reached right
up to the nineteenth century. Such a society is based on
its members providing unpaid work and is supposedly
characterized by the master of the house's right to

discipline the members of the household. The first person to use the discourse of the 'whole', the 'organic house' – the author Wilhelm Heinrich Riehl – described it as follows:

> The organic house had a name, the regular one has a number. In the same way, the old streets that had grown up had their names, which had 'evolved' in the course of history. Newly built streets were given random names. In the most regular town in Germany, Mannheim, they didn't even bother making up names

A copper engraving of the city of Mannheim, Germany, 1758.

for the dead-straight streets, limiting themselves to the simple letters of the alphabet, thus even turning the whole town, as it were, into one big ABC.[11]

You can find the 'whole house' in the writings of feudal lords in the early modern period, however; it has been feeding the fantasies of world-weary historians and nostalgic philosophers ever since the nineteenth century.[12] It came about only due to the administrative activity of Enlightenment 'absolutism' breaking up houses that were already vulnerable by issuing them with a number.[13] This is because the house number made the house visible as subject to a government acting in the name of the state. For the supporters of the 'whole house', however, this is how the government took away the unlimited authority of the master of the house, who would regret losing the 'whole house'. In other words, without a house number there was no such thing as a 'whole house' in the first place.

## In Search of the Origin

In 1929 the venerable journal *Notes and Queries* received the following request: 'When did the present method of numbering houses come into general use?' This query related to London and contributors made a valiant effort to answer it in the subsequent issues. One, for example, knew nothing about London but pointed out that Liverpool was first numbered in 1773. Another contributor claimed that house No. 1 in the Strand was the first to be given a number. Finally the artisan and amateur historian Ambrose Heal set out to answer the query in more detail. He referred to the Acts of Parliament of 1762 and 1765, according to which house signs in London that were considered

House number nought in Strand-on-the-Green, London.

dangerous due to their size had to be taken down and house numbers were to be introduced.[14] In an address book published in 1768, the *Complete Guide*, three-quarters of all the houses named had numbers.[15] In the following

Decorative '70' house number plaque, Lincoln.

decade a German traveller could say of the British metropolis that 'in all the streets of London . . . the houses are designated with numbers . . . a very great convenience that a stranger might wish to see in all large towns.'[16]

It is not surprising that the authors of *Notes and Queries* had so much trouble answering the question about the origin of house numbers. Once house numbers had been introduced and had become accepted, taken for granted in fact, their origins became lost in the mists of time. What is certain is that this whole project of numbering houses can be seen as typical of the eighteenth century. Without any trace of irony, the house number can be considered one of the most important innovations of the Age of Enlightenment, of that century obsessed, as it was, with order and classification. A chronicle of the numbering of houses could begin with the numbering of the houses in the Jewish quarter of Prague in 1727. In the process of what was called the *Judenkonskription*, the 'registration of Jews', not just the houses, but the individual units of habitation within the houses were numbered floor by floor.[17] It would be equally possible to begin with the numbering of the houses in the Paris suburbs in 1724–8, which was carried out in relation to a household census. In this case the numbers were carved into the doorposts. It is true that the numbers were then used for giving addresses, but their actual purpose was not the identification of the houses but the establishment of their number, a total that was not to be added to by putting up new buildings. This numbering of houses was therefore principally a way to restrict the growth of the city; aiding in the search for a house was only a secondary reason.[18] One could also mention that, according to Edward Hatton's *A New View of London* of 1708, the houses of Prescot Street in London were numbered, even if these numbers were not actually used until decades after their appearance.[19]

In the search for the first appearance of this system of addressing one might also include ideas about an urban utopia imagined during the early modern period. For example, in a posthumously published volume by the seventeenth-century architectural theorist Nikolaus Goldmann, *Civil-Baukunst*, which outlines an ideal city, he proposes that 'In every house a number of the door shall be set out in such a manner that one might enquire upon the houses according to their numbers; the number shall be furnished with a place upon which the name of the master of the house might be set out in large letters.'[20]

There were individual cases of numbered houses even in the preceding centuries, however. For example, as early as 1519 the buildings of the Fuggerei, founded by the Fugger family of financiers in Augsburg – a social

House number in the Fuggerei housing complex, Augsburg, Germany.

housing complex that still exists – were said to have been numbered using Gothic numerals. It is a very early occurrence of this system of addressing; if, that is, the numbers were actually used for the identification of the houses.[21] Anyone finally wanting to go further back in search of the origin can point to the 68 houses situated on the Pont Notre-Dame in Paris. These have been consecutively numbered since the fifteenth century, and from as late as the sixteenth century have borne gold numerals on a red background. Jeanne Pronteau, a historian of house numbers, thinks it wrong to see this numbering as a precursor of later house numbering, even though the numbers were actually used for the identification of the houses in records. The purpose of the numbering was not so much to provide the houses with an address as it was to keep a tally of the city's wealth.[22]

And then finally there are myths and legends. How can you find the house of an enemy, particularly if it is situated in a street where all the houses look the same? In the folk tale 'Ali Baba and the Forty Thieves' this is a crucial question.[23] How can the thieves locate the house of Ali Baba's murdered brother Kasim, in which Ali Baba is living, when it is indistinguishable from the other houses? The thief sent on ahead finds a solution: he chalks a small white mark on the house door. Ali Baba's clever slave girl Marjanah discovers the mark and becomes suspicious: it must have been put there by an enemy who is up to no good. Her reaction is to mark all the houses in the street with a similar sign, and hey presto, it works. When the thieves turn up all together to slay Ali Baba, they are confused, not being able to identify the house they are after. Another thief is sent to spy out the house and has the same idea as the first, except that he makes the mark with red chalk in a hidden place. This is to no avail, since Marjanah discovers it once more. Again she makes the same mark on all the doors in the neighbourhood. Once more the thieves arrive at their destination, but this time their captain is furious. He decides to take on the task himself and finds Ali Baba's house:

> Then he observed the house and looked at it attentively. But he didn't need to make any marks, instead he counted the house doors in the street up to the door of the house they were looking for and made a note of the number. In addition he counted

all the corners and windows of the house and
imprinted them so thoroughly on his memory
that he was certain now he could not mistake it.[24]

The number has therefore a crucial role to play and the
thieves are led to the house where Ali Baba is hiding. It is
not marked on the house but is imprinted in the captain's
memory. If it had been chalked on the house, it would
have drawn a great deal of attention. No one who
numbers houses can be up to any good.

But is the tale of Ali Baba just something out of the
*Thousand and One Nights*? By no means. Recent research
has shown that it was only written down and further
embellished at the start of the eighteenth century by
the Orientalist Antoine Galland. The tale was based on
the stories of a Maronite monk. The fact that the captain
of the thieves *counts* the house doors is only mentioned
in a manuscript most likely to have been written at the
beginning of the nineteenth century; that is, in a period
when house numbers had become standard.[25]

## The Triumph of House Numbers: A Gallop through the Eighteenth Century

Looking for the inventor of the house number is probably
a pointless occupation. Karl Marx's statement that 'a critical
history of technology would show how little any of the
inventions of the eighteenth century are the work of a
single individual' would seem to be relevant here.[26] It was
most likely a collective invention introduced at various
times in various places.

It was perhaps Prussia that saw the real start of the
rage for numbering houses. In 1737 a directive was issued

that on the 'day before the military enter small towns . . . numbers are to be posted on the houses', the numbers thus making it easier to provide billets for the army.[27] After the annexation of Silesia and the county of Glatz, numbering was extended to these areas in 1743.[28] In 1752 the introduction of plates with house numbers was decreed: 'in every town, as has already been the case in Silesia, small tin plates with numbers [are to] be prepared by the town council and affixed to the houses.'[29] The numbering was permanent, as is attested to by, for example, an observation by the *Kreishauptmann*, the captain of the district around Znaim (now the Czech town of Znojmo). In answer to an enquiry in 1767 concerning the possible use of house numbering in his district, he stated: 'The said local description and numbering of such houses: which latter, as far as I can ascertain from such as have been seen by my own eyes, confirm that in the royal territories of Prussia these are only to be found in towns, and markets, but not in villages.'[30] Berlin was not yet affected. From Brno in Moravia, on the other hand, it was reported that all the houses situated in the town had been provided 'with tin numerals' since 1744, the areas of the town acting as units for numbering.[31]

House numbers became general all over Europe from the middle of the eighteenth century. It was a period in which those in the service of the police, such as Jacques-François Guillauté, went so far as to propose the numbering of houses for the purpose of surveillance of the population in their nightmarish vision of control.[32] In 1750 or 1751 the houses of Madrid were provided with numbers, and in the process a system of numbering houses by block came into use.[33] The numbers seem to have caught on in Madrid: a British traveller visiting Madrid in the 1770s

confirmed that all the houses had numbers.[34] A few years
after Madrid, it was the turn of Trieste, where in 1754 the
houses were numbered in connection with a census.[35] In
the same year the introduction of house numbering was
discussed in Vienna, but in the end was not carried out.
There was an attempt to sell the new method of control
to the sceptical population by the argument that thereby
'rascally and dangerous folk' could be more easily traced,
but then the authorities prevaricated, possibly out of fear
of too much opposition.[36] The London directives already
mentioned date from 1762 and 1765. In 1766 the houses
were numbered in the German county of Lippe so as to
avoid the addresses of the properties being solely
dependent on house names, which were likely to change.[37]

Numbering was carried out in the Tirol starting in
1767, with numbers painted on the houses in red.[38]
In Innichen the artist Johann Purgmann was given this
task, receiving 3 gulden for the job.[39] In the Habsburg
territories of Further Austria (Vorderösterreich) numbering
was also decreed in 1767.[40] French provincial towns were
given house numbers in 1768 to make it easier to provide
billets for the military. Paris was not affected, since
barracks already existed there, and only in the new
streets round about Les Halles were the houses given
numbers, from 1762.[41] In 1770 house numbering was
decreed in the Bohemian and Austrian lands of the
Habsburg monarchy in preparation for a new army
recruitment system.[42] In the same year in Munich the
painter Franz Gaulrapp was given the task of providing
a set of numbers for each of the four districts of the city,
a police initiative directed against beggars and vagrants,
with the numbers painted in white on the house doors.[43]
A year later (or possibly in 1769) Mainz followed, the six

districts being arranged under the letters A–F. A series of numbers was allotted for the houses of each of the districts and the letter of the section along with the house number (for example, Lit. A 3) was shown above or beside each entrance. Places not given numbers included the Elector's castle, the chancellery building and the barracks, as well as any back buildings that had no access to the street. New buildings were liable to cause a break in the order (for example, D 183 1/4).[44]

In Paris the houses (or rather the doors) were first numbered in 1779, prompted not by the authorities but by a private citizen, Marin Kreenfelt de Storck, editor of the *Almanach de Paris*. To make his address book more efficient, Kreenfelt needed to use addresses based on numbers, at first by means of numbering the lamp posts. He finally hit upon the idea of taking on the task himself. Street by street he painted, or had painted, the numbers above or beside each door, beginning on one side of the street and continuing up to the end, then turning back along the other side, so that the lowest and the highest numbers in the street were opposite one another. Kreenfelt continued with this task until the end of the Ancien Régime, mostly at night – tolerated by the police, but eyed suspiciously by Paris residents – so that his almanac was able to record the numbers against the addresses noted.[45]

In Augsburg, on the other hand, the introduction of street numbers took place in association with the collection for a new poorhouse, providing the collectors of donations with clear districts for their work. One Voch, an engineer, was given this task. The eight municipal districts were arranged according to the letters A–H and the houses were given a series of numbers according to district. The 52 houses of the Fuggerei situated in district G were numbered separately.[46] Geneva was provided with numbers in 1782; Milan (under Austrian rule) received them at the same time as Hungary, in 1786.[47] In the latter, Joseph II was at first confident that the Hungarian nobility would not be opposed to numbering: 'It goes without saying that all the honourable lords, nobles and magnates, whoever they may be, should not be fearful of being recorded along with their families and their castles being numbered just as the royal castle is.'[48] In the edict issued by the royal chancellery in Pressburg (Bratislava) this argument was again employed: nobles and magnates would have nothing to object to in the numbering, 'since the royal and imperial palace itself, inhabited by His Majesty, is similarly numbered'.[49] It turned out differently, however: the ranks of nobles openly objected to the census and its commissioners. Some of the officials were beaten off from villages. One officer was murdered in the county of Veszprém, and another was sprayed with water and made to promise never to set foot in the district again.[50]

The situation was different in Siebenbürgen (Transylvania in modern Romania), where it led to an uprising of the Vlachs (the Romanian peasants). They expected too much from registration – the end of oppression by the local lords – thinking registration was synonymous with recruitment to the military and that therefore it meant the end of their hated service. Those in the uprising were convinced that they were behaving in accordance with Joseph II's wishes, but they were put down.[51]

The registration was also completed by the engagement of the military, and took longer than was planned. The approximately 1,200 official counters employed took well over a year to cover the nearly 8.5 million souls. They started work on 1 November 1784 and the final result was handed over in 4 April 1786; the task had taken a year longer than originally expected by Joseph II.[52] As was the case in the Habsburg hereditary lands, the houses were numbered in black paint. The number had to be three inches high and painted beside or above the doors of houses.[53] A proposal by the county of Komárom to allow a special rule for the houses of nobles – it wanted to demarcate their house numbers in green paint – was not put into practice.[54]

If at first it seemed as though the registration system had been successfully introduced, the ranks of nobles were to win in the end. In particular the high demands for recruitment during the war against the Ottoman Empire in 1788 led to increased opposition. Joseph II had to suspend the new system of recruitment in January 1787. House numbers were taken down from houses against a background of military music being played and cannons being fired.[55]

Meanwhile, in 1787 the author of *Les Liaisons dangereuses*, Pierre Choderlos de Laclos, sent a proposal to the *Journal de Paris* on how one could number the streets of Paris, but had no success.[56] After the Revolution, however, a new system of house numbering was introduced into Paris and other French cities in connection with the levying of a land tax in 1790. It was based this time not on streets, but on districts of the city; as a system of addressing it was a retrograde step compared with Kreenfelt's method. The 48 city districts introduced shortly before, called sections, were given numbers starting from 1. The numbers covered the city in a completely haphazard

One of the most famous house numbers: Cologne 4711, Glockengasse 22–28.

fashion – not unlike places under the Habsburg monarchy – and there were streets on which the houses were painted several times with the same number as they crossed over into different sections.[57]

The French Revolution was important on a European scale as regards house numbers, the Revolutionary Wars bringing house numbering to many towns in Germany, Switzerland and the Netherlands.[58] Mention can be made here of examples such as Aachen in 1794 and Nuremberg in 1796.[59] There is a well-known anecdote from Cologne explaining the name of the eau-de-Cologne firm 4711, according to which, during the French occupation, what was to become the building of the perfume manufacturer Mülhen was given the number 4.711. Numbering had actually been decided upon in Cologne a few days before the French troops marched in. The French then proceeded to put it into practice with a vengeance.[60]

In Berlin house numbering was to be suggested relatively late. In 1798 the police chief Johann Philipp Eisenberg proposed giving the whole city a series of numbers in which the numerals would run continuously in sequence along the houses on the observer's right-hand side.[61] The king of Prussia rejected this method, ordering in 1799 that the numbering should take place street by street. That is what in fact happened, the numbering starting on the right-hand side of the busier or more important part of the street, continuing on the same side up to the end of the street and then running back on the left-hand side.[62]

Finally, in Venice, during the first period of Habsburg rule (1797–1805), the houses were numbered according to districts or *sestieri*. The relevant directive, dated 24 September 1801, ordered that the numbers were to be fixed using black paint made of bone charcoal and oil onto a white painted rectangle already placed on the house. At the same time the street names were written up on the houses and a new land registry of the city districts of Venice was to be set up.[63]

## Opposition and Equality

The summary in the last section does not claim to be complete. It is just an outline of a system of addressing, which could be gone into in more detail. It would be particularly interesting to investigate when house numbers first appeared in colonial cities such as those in Latin America. It might after all be the case that numbering, along with surveillance using fingerprints, started in the colonies and was only later imported into the metropolitan countries from these outlying parts.[64]

What can be said with certainty in the meantime is that the reasons for the introduction of house numbers are probably numerous. They were intended to aid either in billeting the military, or recruiting soldiers. Or else they were introduced to improve the administration of payments and taxes, or fire insurance, or to reduce the number of beggars.[65] All these factors come into play in deciding why houses have been numbered. It is not surprising that what started as a system for military and taxation purposes should give rise to widespread suspicion about this cultural technique. The reaction of people not used to house numbers may be one of horror, as you can see for example from the memoirs of the Swiss Ludwig Meyer von Knonau. Travelling to the University of Halle with his friend Salomon Wyss, he reported: 'When we arrived on Austrian soil . . . we were horrified to see numbers on the houses which appear to us a symbol of the hand of the ruler determinedly taking possession of the private individual.'[66]

As a consequence the numbering of houses has brought about opposition in many places. The 'common folk' regarded the new numbers as symbols of the state and opposed them. In Litomyšl in Bohemia (now the Czech Republic) on the night of 3–4 December 1770 it was alleged that the numbers just put up on the walls of fourteen houses 'were partly befouled with dung, partly gouged out using an iron bar'.[67] This was a violent reaction. What is a house for, after all, if not to protect people from the world by separating them from it? A house is like an extra layer of skin for people, a sort of 'collective clothing'.[68] The dictionary definition of a house is 'in general a place of shelter and safety'.[69] A number fixed to a house positively threatens to rob it of this role of protection. It is a means of getting hold of those men within the house who are capable of military service and recruiting them into the army. A number makes the house visible in the registers of the military authorities, so gouging out the number is an attempt to erase the visibility of the house. Mutilating the house as an extension of the skin could be compared to the acts of self-mutilation carried out by young men of military age trying to avoid military service: cutting off their thumbs or pulling out their teeth in order to make themselves unfit for it. Violence against one's own body, violence against a house – such acts of self-aggression seemed to be all that was left in face of the power of addressing wielded by the state.

Scandalous behaviour similar to what took place at Litomyšl was reported by the district captain in Iglau (present-day Jihlava). On Wednesday, 29 April 1771, census taking and house numbering got under way in Iglau, the main town of the royal district in Moravia. Already on the night of 30 April, however, it transpired 'that a number of unknown miscreants . . . threw detritus at the wall of the Capuchin monastery designated with the number 1° rendering the same totally unrecognizable'. The district captain reacted immediately, summoning 'by beating of the drum' the citizens of Iglau to assemble and calling upon them 'to yield up the scoundrels'. Anyone divulging the names of the culprits was to be given anonymity, their 'name concealed' and in addition given a reward to the sum of 10 imperial thalers. The district captain did not neglect to declare his 'readiness to carry out the most severe threat against this dastardly offence in the event of the discovery of the delinquents'. He recommended that the Moravian governing authorities publicly announce 'an additional punishment for such scoundrels'.[70] The authorities called upon announced that 'this . . . is the first and only case arising to this date in the course of the entire registration in the country, that the inhabitants have responded to the munificent high mindedness of the princely authority with such criminal acts and disobedience, the like of which has not been seen in all the other districts in the land.' There was nothing else to be done: 'should the person or persons responsible be apprehended, they should be handed over to the resident hanging judges for trial.'[71] But according to the surviving documents, nothing of the sort happened: the call for divulging the names of the 'scoundrels' went unheeded and the criminal act unpunished.

Elsewhere in the Habsburg territories of Further Austria we know the name of someone who forcibly removed a house number. In October 1768 in the village of Beuren near Ulm, belonging to the Carthusian monastery of Buxheim, a local barber-surgeon, Johann Georg Wauthier, set about numbering the houses in series. He met with opposition, however, when he came to the house of the cabinetmaker Johann Mayrhoffer. His wife, Franziska Jehlen, shouted to him that 'her husband [had] ordered that when the surgeon came he should be told not to place a numeral on his house.' Wauthier nevertheless proceeded to put the number up. When the house numberer went to the inn that evening, he was called a 'rascal' by the cabinetmaker, who also happened to be there, whereupon Wauthier boxed his ears. This resulted in fisticuffs, in the course of which Wauthier was bitten on the finger and received a foot injury. Into the bargain, Mayrhoffer removed the number from his house. A little later, however, the delinquent seems to have regretted his behaviour, claiming he had been drunk. He requested that the surgeon put back the number. The surgeon told the court official that he forgave Mayrhoffer everything.[72] It is not known whether there were any further consequences for the man who had put up the numbers without so much as a by your leave. One thing is certain: the cabinetmaker achieved renown in the world of drama, becoming the subject of the play *Johann Meyerhofer oder Die Einführung der Hausnummern. Eine Bauernkomödie* (Johann Meyerhofer; or, The Introduction of House Numbers. A Comedy of Peasant Life, 1994) by Manfred Eichhorn.[73]

There was also opposition to house numbers being introduced in Geneva. After two painters there had painted the numbers allocated according to the district of the city, on the night of 21–22 October 1782 as many as 150 numbers were removed in spite of nightly patrols by the military. A suspect named as Françoise Jouard said at her trial that she had regarded the number as something resembling the 'inquisition'.[74]

Even decades after the introduction of house numbers, they were a cause of scepticism. Walter Benjamin for one, in his study of Paris in the nineteenth century, recognized their power, describing the house number as an 'extensive network of controls' that 'since the French Revolution . . . had been bringing bourgeois life ever more tightly into its meshes'. Benjamin knew that the extension of control had not taken place without opposition. In the second half of the nineteenth century the proletarian inhabitants of the Saint-Antoine area still resisted using the 'cold, official number' when giving their addresses, instead preferring to refer to their houses by name.[75]

Even in the twenty-first century it happens that new systems of addressing meet with considerable opposition.

Take, for example, the US state of West Virginia, where until 2001 in rural areas normally only the letter boxes were numbered. These were situated at some distance from the houses, on the side of the highway, giving no indication of their location. The house numbering system newly instituted that year was justified on the grounds of security and was called the '911 addressing system', reflecting the emergency number 911. Unfortunately many property owners were not particularly over the moon about being given a new number. Some of them went beyond shouting about it and threatened the people doing the numbering with rifles and machetes. One member of the Addressing and Mapping Board responsible for numbering the houses came out with the macho comment: 'Addressing isn't for sissies.' The cause of this trouble was that being given a new number was seen as an infringement of people's property and an attack on their identity. One particularly incensed home owner living in Marion County, Ida Starks, wrote to a letters column in 2007 decrying the introduction of the house numbers as evidence of a communist takeover:

> What about our history? This house number means something to me and my family. It means stability, history of both family and community. It means that my work through the years has established my family. Have we become so communist that ownership means nothing? What will they dictate to us next?[76]

Do house numbers mean the dawning of a world of freedom and equality? Well, in past centuries there were people who argued along those lines. It was not just ordinary people who opposed house numbers in the eighteenth century. The nobility also sometimes rose up in arms. Some were not at all in favour of their castles being subjected to numbering, like the humble dwellings of hoi polloi. From their point of view numbering houses was a downright egalitarian act, since all houses were equal before the law of the house number, be they palaces or cottages, stately homes or hovels.

One of those who rose up against it was Graf von Wilczek. When the local commission for numbering in the Stockerau sector in Lower Austria arrived at his castle, Schloss Seebarn, the count prevented them from going about their work and sent the officials packing.[77] The numbering was only achieved when the authority responsible, the Court Council of War, ruled that 'the said castle Sebarn be numbered in a like manner'.[78]

The chronicler of Paris life Louis-Sébastien Mercier was also all too aware of the equalizing effect of house numbers. In 1781 he reported on the fact that in Paris the useful process of house numbering had been brought to a halt. He could only speculate as to the reason: perhaps it was the unwillingness of the nobles to have their entrance gates given numbers. After all, where would we be if the town houses of M. le Conseiller, of the Fermier général, and of his lordship the Bishop were to be given a common or garden number? What would be the point of all those grandiose mansions? Everyone is anxious to keep up appearances. It might even happen that the gate of a house belonging to a noble was given a number following on after a common workshop, suggesting some sort of equality, which should be guarded against at all costs.[79]

## House Numbers and Discrimination against 'Jewish Houses' in the Habsburg Empire

Everyone is equal before the law of the house number, it seems – or are they? Proof of the fact that a house number can also be used as a means of discrimination is provided by the way officials behaved under the Habsburg monarchy. Normally they painted *teutsche* numbers, referring to the Arabic numerals as 'German', on the houses, preceded by the abbreviation 'N' for 'numero' followed by a raised 'o': N°.[80] The fact that the painted number was a house number was thus highlighted by the use of letters. A number on its own was not enough, since it could be confused, in the case of a high number, with a record of the year it was built. In the case of what were called 'Jewish houses' there were special regulations. These were houses owned by Jews (which was generally only possible in the Bohemian territories). They had to be numbered separately and in their case the numbers used were not *teutsche* numbers but Roman numerals.[81] Here the sharp dividing line drawn between Jewish and Christian *souls* was further emphasized. The yellow patch that Jewish men and women had to wear on their clothing in Prague, which was only abolished in 1781, was thus affixed to their houses.[82]

The fact that this differentiation into 'Jewish' and 'Christian' house numbers was adhered to by law is demonstrated by an event that occurred in the town of Turnov, where the owner of 'Adam Hillillisch's Jew's house', designated by the Roman N° XIV, was declared bankrupt. The house became the property of Johann Heinrich Czernisch's heirs, who were Christian. At the same time the *Schutzjude*, or 'Protected Jew', Wolf Löbl bought 'Samuel Etzelerisch's Christian cottage registered under N° 262'. So now Christian souls were living in what was, at least according to the house number, a Jewish house, whereas Jewish souls were living in a Christian house. The town council of Turnov and the district authority of Jungbunzlau (now the Czech Mladá Boleslav) wouldn't tolerate such a confusing situation. They applied to the governing authority of Bohemia for permission to transfer the registration number XIV painted on Hillillisch's former house, which was now the Czernisch house, onto what was formerly Etzlerisch's house, but now belonged to the Jew Wolf Löbl. Vice versa, the number 262 was to be painted on Czernisch's house. There were several reasons for this, one being that nothing had changed as regards the number of Christian houses registered as Jewish houses. In addition, it was stated, 'Czernisch's cottage was entirely isolated from the Jewish houses' and only bordered on houses lived in by Christian souls. Finally, the house bought by Löbl was said to be situated 'among the houses of the Jewish of that place'.[83] The governing authority of Bohemia was persuaded and went along with the 'mixing up' of the numbers, N° XIV becoming 262, 262 becoming XIV.[84] News of this transfer reached Vienna, where it became a subject of debate concerning how far Jews should be allowed to buy houses at all.[85]

Even after the abolition of distinguishing marks for Jews, this differentiation of house numbers remained. House numbers with Roman numerals were used to identify 'Jewish houses' right up until the nineteenth century.[86]

## The Use of House Numbers

Even if house numbers sometimes met with opposition, they were nevertheless often accepted by the population, who appropriated them and used them in everyday life. One can find evidence of this in newspaper advertisements. In the case of Vienna, house numbers were first mentioned in the *Wienerisches Diarium* of 5 January 1771 in an advertisement offering two houses for sale in the Lerchenfeld district – number 24, called Maria Trost, and number 26, called the Green Huntsman – which both belonged to a certain Anton Hölzl.[87]

Immediately after that, on 2 February 1771, an advertisement announced that on 30 January 'a Bolognese puppy, a male white all over and having blue eyes but with one lighter blue than the other and a small muzzle and a black nose, weighing seven pounds' had gone missing. 'Anyone finding or identifying it, should come to No. 222 Bognergasse up to the second floor, and is sure of gaining a good reward.'[88] This announcement of a missing dog used a house number to identify the home to which the dog should be returned. And in fact, on the city map of Vienna produced by Josef Anton Nagel – and the aerial panorama by Joseph Daniel von Huber, the first city plan of Vienna to have the house numbers recorded on it – one can find the house in the Bognergasse.

Another example of the acceptance of house numbers can be found in letters which give precise addresses. In 1781, after being in Vienna for several months, Wolfgang Amadeus Mozart for one was accustomed to giving the house number in his letters so that his correspondents could use it to reply to him. In the case of his first two residences – 'in the *teutschen* [German] house in

Singerstrass [*sic*]' as well as the house called 'Peter im
Aug-gottes [Peter in God's Eye] on the second floor' –
the composer did not mention a house number. But as
early as September 1781 we are told that his new room
was situated 'at N° 1175 the Graben on the third floor'.
The relevant building now has the address number 17
Graben. In 1782 his residence was 'on the high bridge in
the Groshaubts' house N° 387'. The following year it was
'in the small Herbertsteins' house, N° 412 on 3rd floor; chez
Herr von Wezlar', then a little later 'on the Judenplaz in the
Burgs' house, N° 244 on the first floor'. Mozart moved again
in 1784, this time not using any house number in a letter.
Now he was living 'in the Trattners' house, 2nd staircase,
3rd floor', and a little later 'at N° 846 Schullerstrasse, on
the first floor', according to Mozart's father. We also have
his father to thank for Mozart's next address: he 'is now
residing at N° 224 Landstrasse' – in other words, the
composer had moved to the suburbs due to lack of
money. He changed lodgings frequently, living 'in the
Tuchlauben area' and then in the Alsergrund area, 'at
N° 135 Waringergasse at the sign of the three stars'.
He moved from there finally for good to 'N° 970
Rauhensteingasse in the Emperor's house first floor'.[89]
Mozart was truly a restless being, living at no fewer
than twelve addresses during his ten years in Vienna.

Barbara Schönhofer, a citizen of Boschitz in Bohemia
(now Bošice in the Czech Republic), accepted house
numbers in a different way. She was a commoner, who
expressed the wish for a house number on her own
initiative. Her request on 1 May 1784, included in a
purchase contract dated 8 January of the same year,
shows that she was the legal owner 'of an apartment
situated in the house of her brother Ludwig Massizek with

its own entrance'. Her brother's house was identified by the number 50, but the signatory 'is desirous of having a separate *N[ume]ro militari* for herself, wherefore she requests herewith to be granted a separate house *N[ume]ro* for the said purchased apartment by the grace of the inestimable governing authority'. Frau Schönhofer therefore claimed her right to a number. In support of her request she stated that she, along with her husband, had been granted civil rights some years before and had 'served the public with a grocery business throughout eight or more years'. The officials in the governing authority of Moravia and Silesia saw no reason not to grant the grocery lady her wish but wanted to await the decision of the military authorities. This took place in June, and in the opinion of the local recruiting body, there existed 'no objection' to her request, with the only proviso that the section of the house 'as a newly established house be accorded the last numeral in Boschitz in arithmetical order'. Thus any final doubts were dispelled and Frau Schönhofer could be informed that her request for a number had been granted.[90]


**Schramek; or, The Burden of Three Numbers**

August Schramek, a citizen of Brno, had no end of trouble. His story shows how combining building plots and building a new house could cause serious problems and lead to a bureaucratic nightmare.

His first application to the town council of Brno – ending 'Your obedient signatory' – was made in November 1837.[91] He stated that he had erected a new house on the 'building plot purchased from Valentin Falkensteiner', in the neighbourhood of the Ferdinand Gate. When he approached the Registration Office for a number for his new building, he was told to his surprise that his house had to be given three numbers, as three houses had formerly stood on the site. Thus his house was allocated the numbers 421, 422 and 539. Schramek was not at all pleased at this and asked to be given just one. In his first application he justified this on the grounds that he feared 'various disadvantageous effects regarding fees for the owner', by which he presumably meant that he expected to have to pay more tax, assuming that the number of registration numbers allocated was key to tax assessment, rather than the number of existing houses. The request was rejected a few days later. With reference to the registration ruling of 1804, Schramek was informed that his case could only be taken into consideration if there was a complete renumbering of all the houses.

The house owner was not put off, however, and in December he made a new request, arguing that his house was by no means 'situated on the site of three demolished houses'. This was testified to by the site plan drawn up at the time of the demolition and rebuilding of the Ferdinand Gate. He claimed that only a part of the site of the building plot was occupied by his house and in the place of the other two houses the road was now widened. The fact that his house had three numbers had 'led to great confusion because these numbers were too different, people not expecting to find 539 in the vicinity of 421 and 422, thereby causing a very great difficulty, particularly for strangers'. This request was also rejected.

Schramek did not make his next application to the town council but to the district authority of Brno. The result of this was that the building regulation department of the city of Brno was to make a thorough assessment of the situation. According to this, the majority of Schramek's new building was situated on the former site of a deep ditch and what had been used were only three spans of the building plot of the former Number 421 along with four spans of Number 539. The building regulation department supported Schramek's request for one single number. They said that his new building should be given the number 539, while the numbers 421 and 'the numbers of the other houses demolished, 415, 423, 416, 417 and 422, should not fall a burden' on Schramek's house 'but should be used elsewhere for newly built houses'.

Despite the decision of the building regulation department in his favour, Schramek's request to the district authority was ignored. Only when the unused numbers were used for newly built houses on the bastion was there the slightest attention paid to his request. In the meantime, when in 1841 four new houses were built on the bastion, Schramek once more made his request known to the town council. Once again his request was rejected. First, the registration numbers not yet allocated – 417, 418, 419, 421, 422, 423 and 523 – had to be issued to the newly built houses. This time Schramek appealed to the governing authority of Moravia, a legal process that took another two years, until finally on 26 July 1843 permission was at long last granted. With the agreement obtained from the district military command, Schramek was now allowed simply to number his house 539. It had taken almost six years before August Schramek was granted his wish to remove two of the three house numbers.

## Chaos and Resilience: 'Conscription' Numbers under the Habsburg Monarchy

Even more fuss than that caused by such small-scale changes in house numbers has been caused by the renumbering of whole districts or towns. Sometimes this has been necessary. Otherwise the sequence of continuous numbers brought about by new building, combining houses and the demolition of houses, would have got completely out of order. Thus in 1818 the military office in charge of conscription (that is, the registration of people for mainly military purposes) saw it necessary to carry out a renumbering of the city of Brno along with its suburbs. This renumbering was thoroughly welcomed by the town council as regards houses outlying the city but not for the city itself. In the latter case 'a new numbering' was 'to be avoided as much as possible . . . otherwise in future one will not know where one is with the city documents'.[92] Putting it more simply: 'A more frequent new numbering [has] a largely deleterious effect on the city documents by changing numbers in such a short period of time because for no other reason than that future generations will not know the location of a house.'[93] It isn't all that easy to change numbering once it has already been done. A house number is used in too many different ways for it to be easily exchanged for another. Also, the reliability of the postal service might suffer as a result of the renumbering. 'Hence it is the case that in respect to the connections of the inhabitants with other towns and countries a frequent change of numbers would cause confusion in regard of letters.' Instead of renumbering, the town council of Brno therefore favoured a general

tidying up of the house numbers already in existence
so that these could be returned to their former pristine
condition.[94]

The numbers had got into a particularly bad state
in Vienna, where the numbering carried out in 1770 had
already been up and running for a quarter of century. In
1795 there had to be a renumbering for the first time, and
that only lasted for a limited period, as the houses had to
be numbered in sequence all over again in 1821.[95]

The incorporation of the suburbs after 1850, along
with the demolition of the city walls after 1858, made the
problem even worse in Vienna. A solution was announced
in the census law of 1857, according to which 'Numbering
street by street can also be undertaken for the extension
of urban areas.'[96]

'Location' numbers did not usher in the end of
'conscription' numbers. These were still important in
many circumstances, particularly for the land registry list,
and had to be maintained and fixed in the interior of the
houses. It was only after 1874, when the land registry lists
were re-established, that renumbering took place. In everyday
life, admittedly, the conscription numbers were hardly ever
used, in which context it is nevertheless important to mention
that the registration numbers allocated after 1874 in districts
1 to 9 are the same as the numbers entered in the land
registry list; they are still relevant today.[97]

The directive of 24 October 1958, laying down the
appearance of house numbers, is still valid today. The house
number as well as the street name must be given in white
letters on square steel-blue enamel plates. The size of the
plates has to be 33 by 23 cm, and the height of the house
number 11 cm. The writing style used is termed 'lapidary'.[98]
Even in the 1950s it happened that registration numbers

6 Walfischgasse, district 1350, Vienna: a registration number in the form of a location number.

with this design were still being put up on houses, for example at 6 Walfischgasse (N° 1350) or 3 and 5 Freytaggasse (N° 956) in Vienna.

Conscription numbers have proved to be particularly resilient in the Czech Republic. In many towns and villages there they are put up on houses along with location numbers and are still used for a lot of administrative purposes. Identity cards belonging to citizens of the Czech Republic give both numbers as place of residence.[99]

## Mark Twain's Troubles with Berlin House Numbers

The problems just described regarding the chaos of house numbers under the Habsburg monarchy have their root in the fact that the houses there were numbered in sequence according to locality. Such a system is not sufficient for dealing with changes in the composition of the houses, giving rise to more and more criticism towards the end of the eighteenth century. When it came to a debate in Berlin about the best way of numbering the houses there, the Enlightenment author Johann Erich Biester insisted that the method described had 'something disturbing' about it. If the numbers of houses situated opposite one another differed from another by several hundred, it was a case of 'a huge jump that was stretching to the limit any sense of order and the whole idea of coherence'.[100]

Following this reasoning, the houses in Berlin, as mentioned earlier, were numbered street by street. This system can also be tricky, as Mark Twain was to discover when he first stopped in the capital of the Wilhelminian Empire on his tour of Europe in 1891. Twain was enthusiastic about Berlin, regarding it not just as the 'most governed' but the 'best governed city in the world'. Everything seemed to him to be well ordered, for example the fire brigade and the horses and carriages. Only in one respect was there chaos: the numbering of the houses.

At first one thinks it was done by an idiot; but there is too much variety about it for that; an idiot could not think of so many different ways of making confusion and propagating blasphemy. The numbers run up one side of the street and down the other. That is endurable, but the rest isn't. They often use one number for three or four houses – and sometimes they put the number on only one of the houses and let you guess at the others. Sometimes they put a number on a house – 4, for instance – then put 4a, 4b, 4c, on the succeeding houses, and one becomes old and decrepit before he finally arrives at 5. A result of this systemless system is that when you are at No. 1 in a street you haven't any idea how far it may be to No. 150; it may be only six or eight blocks, it may be a couple of miles.

The worst thing, however, for the author of *The Adventures of Tom Sawyer* was the fact that the house numbers were not in sequence but jumped, the number 50 or 60 being suddenly followed by 140 and then descending again. In short, it was 'a sort of insanity' making it difficult to find one's way about in Berlin.[101] The system of numbering houses street by street was no guarantee that chaos and disorder would be held at bay. Madness and confusion emerged the winners again and again in the eternal battle for order and control.

## Odd and Even

The system of house numbering most commonly used in many towns is the one in which even numbers apply to the houses on one side of the street and odd numbers to houses on the other side. This is often referred to as the French system, since it was first introduced in Paris in 1805.[102] According to the latest research, the origin of this method of numbering is not to be found in France, nor even in Europe. There is evidence of this in the travel report from Napoleon's Paris made by the US geographer John Pinkerton. When he was staying there at the start of the nineteenth century, the numbering system based on sections of the city introduced during the Revolution was still in use, making it difficult to find one's way. Pinkerton knew of an alternative: 'The best plan is doubtless that pursued in American cities, which is to give all the odd numbers on one side of the street, and the even on the other, which lends every possible expedition to the research.'[103]

This odd/even system was first used in 1790 in the then capital of the US, Philadelphia. It was US Marshal Clement Biddle who numbered the houses using this method while carrying out a census. Shortly afterwards he published an address book in which he described in detail how to locate any particular house.[104] In the next few years this odd/even system spread to many US cities. In New York, for example, it was introduced in 1793. The numbers were at first made temporarily in chalk, and were then painted on top. Later, tin plates were used.[105]

There is evidence that this system was discussed for the first time in Europe in 1799. In the *Journal de Paris* an engineer called Pierre-Ascension Garros proposed this very method as a better alternative to numbering based on the sections of Paris. In the following years there was a thoroughgoing debate over the pros and cons of the different systems and ways of establishing the numbers. In the end a final decision was made in 1805 during the period of office of Nicolas Frochot, prefect of the département de la Seine. That same year the odd/even system was introduced in Paris and became a model for the whole of Europe.[106]

It sometimes took decades before it was fully established, and there were repeated complaints by city inhabitants who had not been able to find their way because of the difficulty of using the numbering systems. In Vienna, for example, the registration numbering introduced 70 years before was still in use in the middle of the nineteenth century. The journalist Joseph Adami was probably expressing the heartfelt feelings of many

House numbers 35 to 42 on the columns of Georgian houses.

of those frustrated in their quest when he described the difficulty of finding an address in the 'endless sea of houses' in the capital city of the Habsburg monarchy, with its 'totally chaotic' house numbers.[107] It was another fifteen

House number in Zurich 246, Augustinergasse 9.

years before his desire for user-friendly numbering was fulfilled. Not until the decision by the local council on 2 May 1862 was the long-awaited decree issued. One of those who was closely involved with this solution, the entrepreneur Michael Winkler, described the prevailing situation in these terms:

> It is often difficult enough to find an address in a village, a market town, a country town or even in a provincial capital. But finding your way easily and correctly in the metropolis of the Empire, in a capital city of more than 500,000 inhabitants and more than 12,000 irregular house numbers and many intersecting streets and alleys with the same names, is truly an extremely difficult problem. In finding a solution to this extremely complicated task our watchword was very much the practical 'Time is money.'[108]

It is worth mentioning that the cast zinc plates that bore the house numbers and street names were produced by the factory of the same Michael Winkler. He was therefore able to make a lot of money from his work for the city of Vienna. Since the plates were relatively valuable, they were also sometimes stolen, and for that reason, in areas where there was thought to be a danger of this happening, cheap zinc plate was used instead.[109]

Three years after Vienna, Zurich introduced numbering street by street. The new house numbers were called 'police numbers' to distinguish them from the 'fire registry numbers' or 'insurance numbers' that were introduced in connection with fire insurance schemes. The 'directive relating to the numbering of houses on the part of the police' dates from 11 February 1865, stipulating the appearance of the new numbers. Blue plates with white writing 'of appropriate size' were to be put up on the outside walls of houses. This was to be financed by the city. In future, if new numbers were to be put up or damaged ones replaced, house owners would be required to pay a sum of 1½ Swiss francs. The insurance numbers were retained but they were moved to another position, such as the entrance. Nowadays they are sometimes to be found inside the doors.[110]

It took even longer in Berlin, where Mark Twain described the chaos so graphically. The new system, which was called the 'alternate side numbering sequence', was not introduced until 1929. However, for economic reasons complete renumbering of all the streets did not take place. Today in Berlin there are still two numbering systems, which drives visitors crazy.[111]

## Methods of Numbering

Aside from the odd/even system, human ingenuity has come up with a surprising variety of ways of numbering houses, which can each be differentiated in the following ways:[112]

*Numbering in sequence according to place*
This was used, for example, under the Habsburg monarchy. Starting with a house at the entrance to a place or with a seat of the nobility (for example, the Hofburg Palace in Vienna or the Castle in the Hradčany in Prague) there was a sequence of numbers counting from one. The last house numbered was given the highest number. In towns this could reach quite a large number, sometimes going into four figures. If one was in a hurry to find a location, it could only be identified by adding the street name.

Hradčany 1, detail of the entrance to Prague Castle at the Matthias Gate.

Fondaco dei Tedeschi, San Marco 5562, Venice.

*Numbering in sequence according to district*
In towns such as Mainz, Augsburg and Nuremberg a
letter was allocated to each district of the town and the
houses within the districts were numbered in sequence.
The letter of the district was often put up on the house in
addition to the number. Thus in Nuremberg, for example,
where numbering was carried out in 1796 at the behest
of the French occupation forces to simplify the billeting of
the military, the houses in the two districts around St Sebald
and St Lorenz had the house numbers S1 to S1706 and L1
to L1578 painted on the fronts respectively.[113] In Venice
such a system – but without the allocation of a letter for
each *sestiere* – has been in use right until the present, so
it's something of a challenge to find a house in that city
on the Lagoon.[114]

*Numbering according to block*

This was less common than the two other methods mentioned so far. Here a combination of numbers and letters were allocated to a block and the houses of this block were given a series of numbers. In Madrid, for example, a separate number was allocated to every block of houses (called *manzana*) surrounded by streets and the houses of the block were numbered based on this. To locate an address it was therefore necessary to know the street name and the number of the block as well as the number of the house in the block.[115] In the centre of the town of Mannheim a similar system is still in use today, with every block of houses being allocated a letter and a number (for example, A1 or U6). Here the houses of every block are numbered either clockwise or anti-clockwise, a typical address being B2,5 or U7,3.

Numbering by block in Mannheim.

*Manzana* numbering in Madrid.

*Horseshoe numbering by street (the clockwise scheme)*
A sequence of numbers, always beginning with 1, is allocated to each street. This goes up one side of the street and back down the other until the house with the highest number in the street is opposite the lowest. In Switzerland this system is also called 'boustrophedon numbering', that is, numbering on alternate sides.[116] This method was used by Kreenfelt de Storck in Paris in the 1770s, among others. It was taken up in Berlin in 1799–1801 and is still partly in use there today.

*The alternate odd/even system*
With this system numbers are also allocated by street but the houses on one side of the street are numbered using only even numbers, and on the other side using odd numbers. This method spread from the USA (Philadelphia,

1790) via Paris (1805) to many European towns. In Vienna (1862) it was called 'location numbering'.

*The block decimal system*
This was first used in Philadelphia. Here after 1856, 100 numbers were dedicated to the houses of every block in a street. From the next intersection the numbering started with the next hundred, so that you get houses with four- or five-figure numbers. This system was known as the Philadelphia system.[117]

*The metric system (the distance scheme)*
With this the number given to a house is decided by the distance of the house from a defined zero point. The 'Numérotation métrique' worked out by the mathematician Auguste-Savinien Leblond as early as 1800 is used in many French localities. A similar system is also in place in Latin America.[118]

*The decametric system*
This is a mixture of the alternate and the metric numbering methods in which the numbers are decided as in the last method, according to the distance from the starting point, but odd and even numbers are used on opposite sides. Designed by the architect Jean-Jacques Huvé, it has been introduced in the last few decades, particularly in countries in sub-Saharan Africa.[119]

**House Numbers and Colonialism at Home**

In the nineteenth century it was still far from the case that houses were numbered everywhere in Europe. The introduction of house numbering was very difficult for the authorities, particularly in outlying areas. In his novel *The Bridge on the Drina* Ivo Andrić describes how in around 1850 an attempt was made to introduce house numbers at Travnik in Bosnia under the Turks:

> Thirty years ago, if not more, there was a Vezir in Travnik, a certain Tahirpaša Stambolija. He was one of the converted, but false and insincere. He remained a Christian in his soul, as he had once been . . . It was this Tahirpaša who began to number the houses in Travnik and on each house he nailed a tablet with the number (it was for this reason that he was known as 'the nailer'). But the people rebelled and collected all those tablets from the houses, made a pile of them and set fire to it. Blood was about to flow for this, but luckily a report of this reached Stambul and he was recalled from Bosnia. May all trace of him be abolished!

Habsburg colonial power was hardly more successful in this regard. In 1878, the first year Bosnia was occupied, a start was made to carry out a census and house numbering. According to Andrić's description the population knew only too well that this was the prelude to the exploitation of people in the form of compulsory labour or military service. For this reason the religious dignitary Alihodža makes the following proposal:

> If you ask me what we should do, this is my opinion. We have not got the army to rise at once in revolt. God sees that and all men know. But we do not have to obey all that we are commanded. No one need remember his number nor tell his age. Let them guess

when each one of us was born. If they go too far and interfere with our children and our honour, then we shall not give way but will defend ourselves, and then let it be as God wills!'

Andrić continues:

They went on discussing the unpalatable measures of the authorities for a long time, but in the main they were in agreement with what Alihodža had recommended: passive resistance. Men concealed their ages or gave false information, making the excuse that they were illiterate. And as for the women no one even dared to ask about them, for that would have been considered a deadly insult. Despite all the instructions and threats of the authorities the tablets with the house numbers were nailed upside down or hidden away in places where they were invisible. Or else they immediately whitewashed their houses and, as if by chance, the house number was whitewashed too. Seeing that the resistance was deep-seated and sincere, though concealed, the authorities turned a blind eye, avoiding any strict application of the laws with all the consequences and disputes which would inevitably have ensued.[120]

Even at the start of the twentieth century many areas on the fringes of the Habsburg empire were without house numbers. This is confirmed by Joseph Roth in his novel *The Radetzky March*. The protagonist of the novel, Carl Joseph von Trotta, when stationed a few years before the outbreak of the First World War on the Russian border, makes the following observation: 'The streets had no names and the little houses no numbers, and anyone looking for a particular place had to follow whatever proximate directions he was offered. This fellow lived behind the church, that one opposite the town gaol, a third past the District Court. It was just like living in a village.'[121]

The ability of states to influence where their writ runs was therefore limited by the lack of house numbers, particularly in areas like those mentioned here, in Bosnia or Galicia, which could be considered to have been colonies.[122]

## Photographing House Numbers around 1900

House number photography can be regarded as the deliberate photographing of house numbers with the objective of documenting them. One of the earliest known examples of this rather rare form of photography was carried out in Paris in 1900 by the Commission Municipale du Vieux Paris. At a meeting of this commission a written paper was delivered by a certain Monsieur Vial, vice-president of the Société Historique et Archéologique 'Le Faubourg Saint-Antoine', who had noted that some of the house numbers that had been introduced in 1726 still existed in that faubourg. The commission thereupon decided to check the details and sent a delegation to the addresses named by Vial. It was true that the old numbers could be found engraved in stone at the places indicated: at 30 rue de Charenton there was the number 6 and at 161 rue de Charonne the number 32. In the case of the latter, admittedly, the actual inscription was not the original but had been redone after restoration of the gateway. At 61 rue des Boulets they

Example of an engraved house number dating from 1726 at 139 rue de Charonne, Paris.

Example of an engraved house number dating from 1726, the number 6 at 30 bis rue de Charenton, Paris.

found the number 3, at 61 rue de Picpus the number 14 in a poor state of repair, and at 30 rue Basfroi the number 4. Apart from the numbers identified by Vial they found some others: 6 at 98 rue de Charonne, 25 at 139 rue de Charonne and 11 at 53 rue de Picpus. It was then decided to have the numbers photographed. Attached to the report of the meeting is a photo of the gateway to 98 rue de Charonne with the number 6.[123] Naturally it would be interesting to do some research into what happened to those photos, since the Commission Municipale du Vieux Paris still exists.

Today, however, hardly any of the numbers that existed in 1900 survive. I was able to identify only the number 6 at 30 bis rue de Charenton and 25 at 139 rue de Charonne along with 32, which was originally at 161 in the same street. The gateway had been transferred at the time of demolition of the building, together with its number, next to 24 passage Courtois.

### Green and Golden House Numbers: The House Number as a Mark of Distinction

Creating a special house number to highlight a particular quality of the house's owners – such as the previously mentioned attempt in Hungary to introduce green numbers to identify the residences of the nobility – is not peculiar to the eighteenth century. Even in the twentieth century there were examples of such a tendency, including in the former East Germany. Golden house numbers were allotted to particularly outstanding households that had beautified their houses or gardens. These were awarded on the basis of a competition organized by the local council of a town or district, together with the communist National

A golden house number at Karl-Marx-Allee 106, Berlin.

Front of the German Democratic Republic.[124] After the fall of the Berlin Wall in 1989, the awarding of this distinction fell largely out of use, but it was later reintroduced in many places, for instance in Neutrebbin in 1995. A local newspaper, the *Märkische Oderzeitung*, reported that a family in Neutrebbin, a locality in the federal state of Brandenburg, was awarded a golden house number in November 2008 for the thirteenth time in a row following a 'Most Beautiful Property' competition.[125] Even in conservative Bavaria a 'golden house number' was introduced in 2003. It is awarded every two years in the district of Straubing-Bogen as a prize in a house building competition, promoting 'sustainable home building', by which the awarding body means 'reflecting the local building heritage and enhancing the typical image of the local landscape'. What is opposed to here is any fashionable or alien influences creeping into the heart

Green house number at Weisse Gasse 6, Erfurt.

of traditional Bavaria, such as 'patio paving slabs . . .
imported from India or China', 'Italianate villas' or 'leylandii
hedging'. All such 'tendencies towards globalization' are
to be avoided.[126]

In recent German history there have also been
examples of green house numbers, which have been
awarded to eco-friendly buildings first in the Saarland,
then in Mainz and Erfurt. The criteria are laid down in
the local building regulations: the more environmentally
friendly the construction of a house is, the more eco
points it is awarded. Installing a solar-powered water
heater on the roof earns you eighteen points, for example.
When you reach 100 points, you can claim a green house
number. The first was awarded to a terraced house in the
Kohlhof district of Neunkirchen in June 1996.[127]

The idea of introducing such an award hasn't always
been greeted with approval. When the Greens on the

town council of Worms wanted to create an award for environmentally friendly building in October 2005, they met opposition. According to a newspaper report, Gerhart Schnell, a representative of the Christian Democrats, saw in it 'a great risk of making a distinction between good and less good people'. Besides that, the administration costs would be much too high. Ernst-Günter Brinkmann from the Social Democrats also had objections, seeing in it 'the risk of "stigmatization and labelling"'. He predicted that anyone active in social affairs would in future be given a red house number; a black one would be for a Christian; anyone in business might receive another colour. 'This is just not on', Brinkmann told the Greens.[128]

The exterior of a house thus occupies a precarious position between the public and the private. Any clear hints as to the interior, whether the style of building or the taste of those living there, can be seen as problematic.

## House Numbers and Superstition

There is a word for the superstitious fear of the number thirteen: triskaidekaphobia. The phobia was identified in the late nineteenth century and extends to house numbers. It's the reason why a property owner in Berlin in 1910 applied to the city council to have house number 13 changed to 12a – he was missing out on tenants thanks to the unlucky number.[129] Nancy Reagan, who was notorious for dabbling in astrology and numerology, was beset by similar fears after friends of her husband bought a house in Bel-Air in 1986 with the idea that she and her husband would live in it after the end of his presidency. Its address was 666 Saint Cloud Drive. Living in a house with what the Bible would term the 'number of the beast' was more than the First Lady could stomach and she managed to have the number changed to 668.[130]

By the end of the twentieth century this sort of superstition had gone global. House numbers have not been spared the heady brew of New Age religion and numerology. Anyone surfing Internet forums will soon discover that now there is a dangerous new house number: 4. Houses blessed with this number have bad feng shui, as number 4 means death according to Chinese superstition. This can even be seen reflected within the European tradition, in view of the fact that the two digits of unlucky number 13 added together equal 4. What are you supposed to do, then, if you are moving to a house with the number 4? This was the question asked by someone with the nickname Pole Star, a concerned contributor to an Austrian New Age forum in August 2004. There were just four (!) answers to the enquiry. One was that a little 'b' could be secretly added to the number – but this might cause a problem with the authorities. Another suggestion was that the negative energy could be made positive by means of an Om symbol, but this raised the question whether it would be better to display this on the inside or the outside of the house. Another was to display a lucky double eight in rainbow colours next to the troublesome number. Finally there was a suggestion that a red circle should be drawn around the 4 to protect against harmful radiation. In this last case, however, the contributor was still left with a problem: what should he or she do if the house is allocated the number 4 but the number isn't displayed anywhere?[131]

1A Ballhausplatz, Vienna: the house number of the 'Embassy of concerned citizens', December 2001.

## The Right to an Address

It is often the case that social movements are opposed to any control or surveillance systems – and house numbers can be included within these. But sometimes the reverse is true. Take for example a moment in the recent history of Austria. On 9 February 2000 protests were held on the Ballhausplatz, where the Federal Chancellery and the President's Office are situated in Vienna, against the formation of a coalition government by the ÖVP, the conservative Austrian People's Party, and the FPÖ, the far-right Freedom Party of Austria. Protestors erected an 'Embassy of concerned citizens'; first a tent, then a container were used as the centre for the opposition to the unpopular government. This became the rallying point for the demonstrations, which took place every Thursday. The unique movement claimed the right to have an address, at the beginning of March 2000 going so far as to allocate itself a house number, 1A Ballhausplatz.[132] This location was given as a contact address by Radio Reverberation, a programme broadcast by the alternative Radio Orange. On the homepage there was the added comment: 'registered mail is guaranteed delivery'.[133] Having an address therefore doesn't just mean the possibility of being forced to join up or pay taxes. On occasion it's something to be desired. Control and surveillance systems are more likely to be implemented if they can be used by those affected for their own purposes. After being broken up in April 2002 and bringing their activity to an end voluntarily in September of the same year, the Embassy in fact saw a revival in June 2003. It started up at a new location, this time by the Danube Canal – and without an identifying house number.[134]

## Taking Over the World: House Numbers in the Twenty-first Century

Even in the twenty-first century there are still towns where house numbers aren't used every day. Tokyo is a well-known case, a city 'with no address', as Roland Barthes called it. It is true that there is a house numbering system there based on the block in which a residence can be found, but it is not used to locate buildings. Instead of identifying the street name and the house number, the address is often represented in the form of sketches, by hand or printed, giving the directions to a residence from a starting point such as a railway station. If you are looking for a place and don't happen to have a drawing, you just go to the nearest local police booth and there you are given the necessary information.[135]

But places without house numbers are getting rarer. Continent after continent has been taken over by numbers. In the middle of the 1980s a large-scale project of cooperation was launched between the World Bank and the French Ministry of Foreign Affairs. Between 1989 and 1994 the larger towns in fifteen states in sub-Saharan Africa, including countries such as Benin, Cameroon, the Republic of Congo, Mozambique and Senegal, were given house numbers, generally using the decametric system. Reviewing the project, the town planners put a figure of approximately $200,000 on the cost of introducing a system of addresses for each of the larger towns and emphasized that this measure could bring about 'slum upgrading'.[136] In around 2005 the German architect Michael Maiwald was given the task by the Frankfurt Centre for International Migration and Development (CIM) of introducing street names and house numbers in the 3 million-strong metropolis of Addis Ababa. A newspaper article about this plan described how paying electricity bills had been achieved until that time: 'The Ethiopian telephone service, the water and electricity systems too are awaiting the introduction of addresses. So that then they will be able to send out their bills. Until now people have been coming with their cash once a month to a collection point where they can pay their bills. Anyone not coming and paying has their water, telephone and power cut off.'[137] The cost of allocating the house numbers – they are allocated by street, according to the alternate side numbering system – was covered by the house owners and was around $5.[138] At the same time another team of German geographers from the University of Heidelberg were working on a Geographical Information System, including house numbers and postal codes, for the emirate of Ras al-Khaimah.[139]

Finally, in South Korea the system of house numbering by block introduced in 1918 by the Japanese colonial powers was replaced in 2014 by a system of alternate side numbering. In all, 160,000 street names and more than 5 million house numbers had to be allocated.[140] The triumphal march of house numbers therefore continues unabated in the twenty-first century. In the age of aerial photography and geo-information systems, there is no stopping the process by which every house is known to the beady eyes of the authorities. But is it just the authorities? No such luck. Internet firms too have an interest in getting hold of your address and knowing your house number. In 2012 Google started to transcribe house numbers photographed by their Street View using their very own reCAPTCHA user-dialogue system. People using Google were therefore helping Google to refine their products free of charge.[141] It will be interesting to see how people handle this new situation, and what strategies of appropriation and subversion they will employ against it.

Example of a Golden House Number in the DDR Museum Pirna, Germany.

House number 1 in Bolzano (Bozen) in the South Tyrol province of Italy.
Above it is the city coat of arms.

16–17 Malostranské Naměstí, Malá Strana, Prague 1.

Neue Schloss (new castle) in Gmünd, Carinthia.

Spiegelgasse 1, Zurich, home of the Cabaret Voltaire, where members of the Dada movement performed in 1916.

The French philosopher Gilles Deleuze's house number, 1 bis rue de Bizerte, Paris.

2 Louis Vincent Street, Jerusalem.

Door in Lüneburg, Germany. Stained glass window with two smelts, symbols of the city.

Detail of the stained glass house number in Lüneburg, Germany.

House number plate with the old 'conscription' number and the new 'orientation' number in Guntramsdorf, Austria.

House number in Forst, Baden-Württemberg, Germany.

House number in Hong Kong: Chai Wan Kok Catholic Primary School, On Yin Street.

Gothic entrance to a former monk's cell in a monastery cloister in Karthaus, South Tyrol.

House number on boulevard Saint-Michel, Paris.

House number on rue de Rivoli, Paris.

Prandtauerstrasse 4, 3100 Sankt Pölten, Austria.

House number in Marrakech, Morocco.

Pod Vyšehradem 5, Podolí, Prague.

Rue Roger Verlomme, Paris.

Where the writer Karl Kraus lived: Lothringerstrasse 6, Vienna.

An old house number 6 in Nishapur, Iran.

Ballgasse 8, district 1343, Vienna.

House number 8, St Michael's Monastery in Jaffa, a Greek Orthodox patriarchate with a blue metal door and letters. The plaque has Greek, English and Arabic inscriptions: 'ΙΣΧΣ ΝΙΚΑ' means 'Jesus Christ Conquers'.

The number 9 is a 2-ton sculpture by Ivan Chermayeff. Solow Building, 9 West 57th Street, New York.

Rue Lebouis, Paris.

10 Downing Street, the British Prime Minister's residence.

Where the German philosopher Walter Benjamin lived from 1938 until 1940:
10 rue Dombasle, Paris.

House number 10 in Schwetzingen, Germany, with an asparagus decoration at the entrance.

Letter box in Neidenstein, Germany.

10 bis rue Lamartine, Paris.

11 boulevard Arago, Paris. House number integrated in the decorative facade, dating from the second half of the 19th century.

House number in the new and old version, in Amman, Jordan.

Ceramic piece by Margit Kovács on a Régiposta Street building designed by Lajos Kozma,
Budapest, 1930s.

Rue Ernest et Henri Rousselle, Paris.

Spiegelgasse 14, Zurich: Lenin lived here, nearly opposite the Cabaret Voltaire, from 1916–17.

Where the historian Eric Hobsbawm grew up: Vinzenz Hess-Gasse 14, Vienna.

House number 15 in Chiwa, a city in Uzbekistan.

House number in Baden-Württemberg, Germany.

*previous:* Ceramic house number in Germany.

15 Place du Général de Gaulle, Chartres, France. Gothic revival keystone and house number.

A house name, sign and number by district and street as well as year number: Heuberg 17, Basel 424.

House number '17' in Germany.

Bangkok, Thailand.

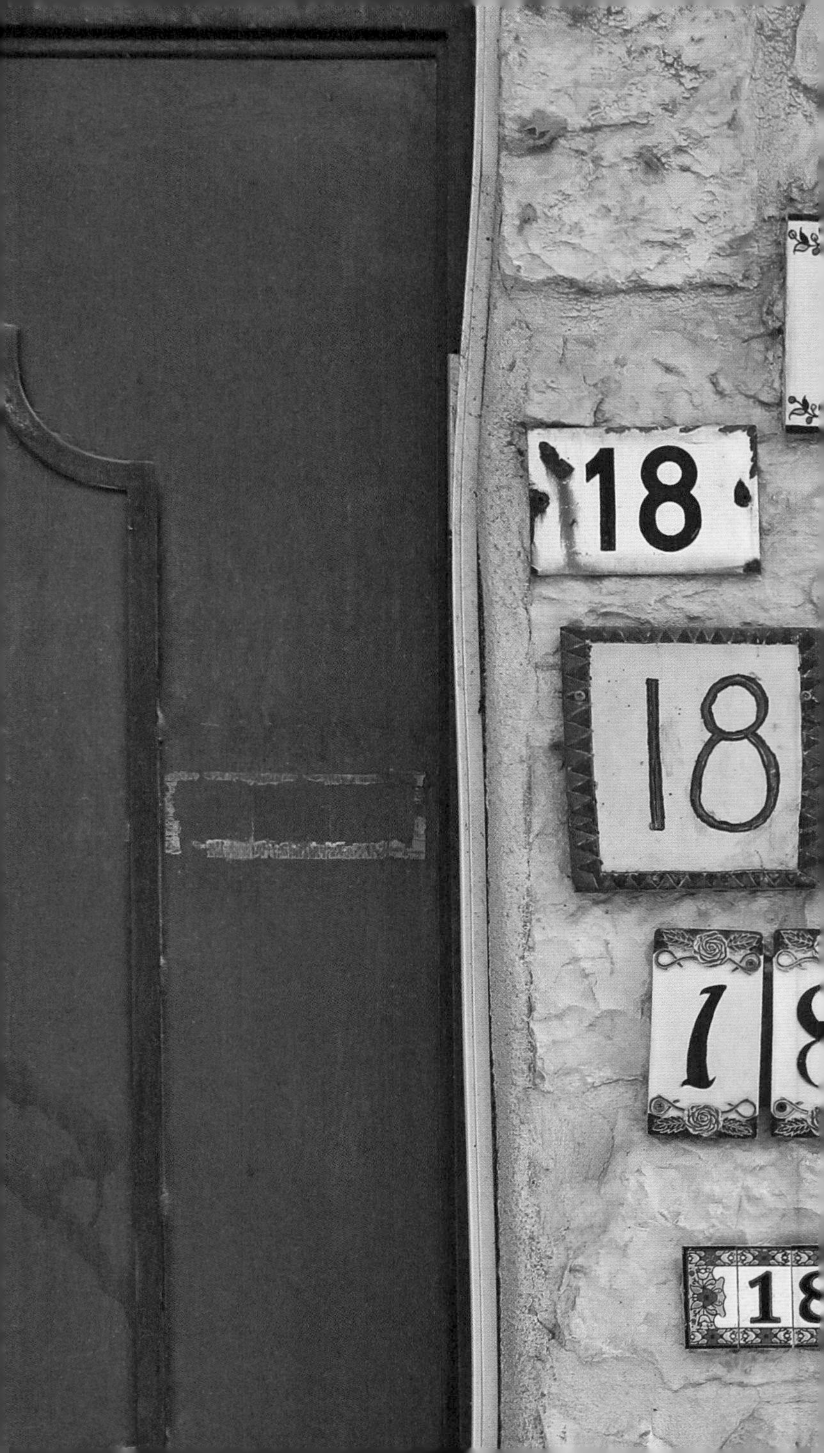

18
18
18
18

*previous:* Jerusalem, Rama Street. The number 18 is auspicious in Hebrew because it is the value of the word חי, meaning life.

A blue house number with vine, Rheinland-Pfalz, Germany.

House number with subdivision in Yerevan, Armenia.

Sigmund Freud's residence in Vienna: Berggasse 19, 9th district.

20 Maresfield Gardens, London, where Sigmund and Anna Freud lived in exile.

Number 21 in front of the Bata's skyscraper in Zlín, Czech Republic.

An 8-m-high number 22, Hörrde-Clarenberg, Germany.

Example of renumbering: 22 square Alboni, Paris.

22 Abovyan Street, Yerevan, Armenia.

Wielandstrasse 23, Berlin, where Rosa Luxemburg lived around 1900.

House number 23, Unter der Metzig, Ulm, Germany.

Lisburn Street, Hillsborough, County Down, Northern Ireland.

A stone number plaque carved with tumbling men, women and monkeys.

Bolzano (Bozen), Italy.

House number 28 in the town of Rheinzabern, Germany.

Via Appiani house number, neighbourhood of San Francesco, Italy.

The narrowest house in Europe at 57 cm wide, in the historic centre of Bregenz, Vorarlberg, Austria.

Wiener Strasse 36, in Sankt Pölten, Austria.

37 Sehit Mehmet Paşa sokak (street), Istanbul.

Bandgasse 11, district 39, Vienna.

Boulevard Richard Lenoir, Paris.

Sickingenstrasse 41, Berlin.

House number 47, Germany.

8 passage Jean-Claude Godfrain (formerly 49 rue de Maubec), Toulouse, France.

Plaque with house number in Córdoba, Spain.

House number in the so-called Sonnenwohnheim, a home for working women in
Hufelandstrasse, Nürnberg. Built 1955–7 by William Schlegtendal.

55 Public Square in downtown Cleveland, Ohio.

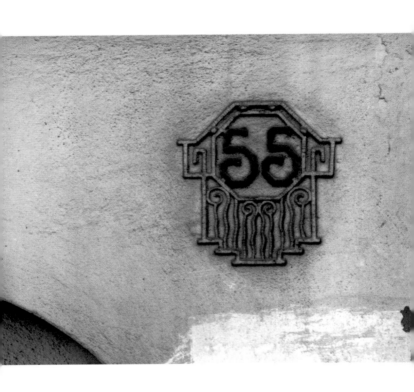

Rue Brancion, Paris.

House number with Tibetan and Chinese street identification, Gyangze, Tibet.

SAN FRANCISCO
JAVIER

64

*previous:* A painted tile of Saint Francis Xavier, next to the street numbers of a house. The streets in Old San Juan, Puerto Rico are named after saints, who appear on the houses on painted tiles.

Hebrew house number 65 in Batei Ungarin, Jerusalem.

Goethe's house, Am Frauenplan 2, Weimar.

Rue de l'Ouest, Paris.

Friesenheim, Germany.

Boulevard de Sébastopol, Paris.

Štěpánkova, Chrudim, Czech Republic.

Rue de l'Université, Paris.

95 Mahmud Koshgariy Street, Samarkand, Uzbekistan.

An underground house number in the Musée des égouts de Paris (Paris Canal Museum).

Rue de la Convention, Paris.

Loretánská 19, 104 Hradčany, Prague.

House number 109, Antequera, Spain.

House number 111, Antequera, Spain.

116 North Rockingham Avenue, Los Angeles where the Austrian composer Arnold Schönberg lived in exile.

Sigmund Freud's birthplace in Příbor.

Calle Mercaderes no. 120, Havana.

Kettenhofweg 123, the philosopher Theodor W. Adorno's house in Frankfurt.

Chausseestrasse 125, Berlin, where Bertolt Brecht lived.

Cité Constitución 135, Barrio Bellavista, Santiago.

157

House number and sea view outside a residential house, Marine Drive, UK.

Sněmovní 158, in the Lesser Town (Malá Strana), Prague.

Rue de la Convention, Paris.

Commemorative plaque above a house number in Casa Esquerre, Concepción, Chile.

Unusual street number of 184¾ in New York City.

Mittelbadgasse 200, Lit. C. 38, Heidelberg, Germany.

224 Thamel, Kathmandu.

The philosopher Michel Foucault's house: 285 rue de Vaugirard, Paris.

House numbers on the corner of K Hošti and Zahradní streets, Kostelec nad Černými lesy, Prague.

# N.º 365

Tržiště 365/15, Malá Strana, Prague.

Steindlgasse 4, Vienna, 1st district 1242 (previously 429).

Michalská 19, Old Town (Staré Město), 436 Prague.

No. 553, Husova 18, Staré Město, Prague.

Registration number 171 at Koroška cesta 12, Maribor, Slovenia.

Rectangular stepping stones leading to a modern house.

First District 1379, Köllnerhofgasse 3, Vienna.

A mailbox in Ruston, Louisiana, decorated with the American flag.

House number and numbered street in Cienfuegos, Cuba.

Calle del Dose, Venice.

# References

1 Michel Foucault, *Discipline and Punish: The Birth of the Prison*, trans. Alan Sheridan (New York, 1995), p. 213.

2 Joachim Eibach, 'Das offene Haus. Kommunikative Praxis im sozialen Nahraum der europäischen Frühen Neuzeit', in *Zeitschrift für Historische Forschung*, XXXVIII (2011), pp. 621–64.

3 Roger Ling, 'A Stranger in Town: Finding the Way in an Ancient City', in *Greece and Rome*, XXXVII (1990), pp. 204–14; Paavo Castrén, '*Vici* and *insulae*: The Homes and Addresses of the Romans', *Arctos: Acta Philologica Fennica*, XXXIV (2000), pp. 7–21.

4 Julia Hillner, 'Die Berufsangaben und Adressen auf den stadtrömischen Sklavenhalsbändern', *Historia*, L (2001), pp. 193–216.

5 Daniel Lord Smail, *Imaginary Cartographies: Possession and Identity in Late Medieval Marseille* (Ithaca, NY, and London, 2000), pp. 220f.

6 David Garrioch, 'House Names, Shop Signs and Social Organization in Western European Cities, 1500–1900', *Urban History*, XXI (1994), pp. 20–48; Georg Simmel, *Soziologie: Untersuchungen über die Formen der Vergesellschaftung* (Frankfurt, 1992), pp. 711–15.

7 *Wiener Schildregister, oder Anweisung, wie man sich auf der Stelle helfen kann, wenn man in Wien den Schild eines Hauses oder eines Kaufmannsgewölbes in und vor der Stadt suchen, und ihn finden will* (Vienna, [1795]), pp. 4–5.

8 Garrioch, 'House Names', pp. 34f.

9 Michael Mitterauer and Reinhard Sieder, *The European Family: Patriarchy to Partnership from the Middle Ages to the Present*, trans. Karla Oosterveen and Manfred Hörzinger (Oxford, 1982), pp. 7–11 (p. 10).

10 See for example Otto Brunner, 'Das "ganze Haus" und die alteuropäische "Ökonomik"', in Otto Brunner, *Neue Wege der Verfassungs- und Sozialgeschichte* (Göttingen, 1968), pp. 103–27; Claudia Opitz, 'Neue Wege der Sozialgeschichte? Ein kritischer Blick auf Otto Brunners Konzept des "ganzen

Hauses'", *Geschichte und Gesellschaft*, XX (1994), pp. 88–98; Valentin Groebner, 'Ausser Haus. Otto Brunner und die "alteuropäische Ökonomik'", *Geschichte in Wissenschaft und Unterricht*, XLVI (1995), pp. 69–80; Hans Derks, 'Über die Faszination des "Ganzen Hauses'", *Geschichte und Gesellschaft*, XXII (1996), pp. 221–42.

11 Wilhelm Heinrich Riehl, *Die Familie* (Stuttgart, 1855), p. 184.

12 The world-weary view of Jean-François Lyotard in relation to the 'domus' seems very similar to Brunner's elegy to the 'whole house': Jean-François Lyotard, 'Domus and the Megalopolis', in Jean-François Lyotard, *The Inhuman: Reflections on Time*, trans. Geoffrey Bennington and Rachel Bowlby (Stanford, CA, 1991), pp. 191–204.

13 On the vulnerability of the house: Richard van Dülmen, *Kultur und Alltag in der frühen Neuzeit*, vol. I: *Das Haus und seine Menschen 16. – 18. Jahrhundert* (Munich, 1990), p. 12.

14 P.D.M.: 'Street Numbers in London', *Notes and Queries*, CLVI (1929), p. 264; Ambrose Heal, 'Street Numbers in London', *Notes and Queries*, CLVI (1929), pp. 354f.; see also Penelope J. Corfield, 'Walking the City Streets: The Urban Odyssey in Eighteenth-century England', *Journal of Urban History*, XVI (1990), pp. 132–74 (p. 150).

15 Ambrose Heal, 'The Numbering of Houses in London Streets', *Notes and Queries*, CLCCCIII (1942), pp. 100–101 (p. 100).

16 Gebhard Friedrich August Wendeborn, *Beyträge zur Kenntnis Grosbritanniens vom Jahre 1779* (Lemgo, 1780), p. 242.

17 Jaroslav Prokeš and Anton Blaschka, 'Der Antisemitismus der Behörden und das Prager Ghetto in nachweissenbergischer Zeit', *Jahrbuch der Gesellschaft für Geschichte der Juden in der Čechoslovakischen Republik*, I (1929), pp. 42–262 (p. 259, n. 16).

18 Jeanne Pronteau, *Les Numérotages des maisons de Paris du XVe siècle à nos Jours* (Publications de la sous-commission de recherches d'histoire municipale contemporaine, VIII) (Paris, 1966), pp. 71–9; see also Walter Benjamin, *The Arcades Project*, trans. Howard Eiland and Kevin McLaughlin, ed. Rolf Tiedemann (Cambridge, MA, and London, 1999), p. 521.

19   Heal, 'Numbering', p. 100.

20   Nicolaus Goldmann, *Vollständige Anweisung zu der Civil Bau-Kunst . . .*, ed. Leonhard Christoph Sturm (Wolffenbüttel, 1696), pp. 111–14 (p. 113).

21   Otto Nübel, *Die Fuggerei* (Augsburg, 2000), p. 16.

22   Pronteau, *Numérotages*, pp. 61–9.

23   'Die Geschichte von Ali Baba und den vierzig Räubern', in *Die Erzählungen aus den Tausendundein Nächten*, trans. Enno Littmann, 12 vols (Frankfurt, 1976), vol. IV, pp. 791–859 (pp. 826–34, 845f.); for the translation from the Arabic (see vol. XII, p. 650) Littmann used a manuscript edited in 1910 by Duncan B. MacDonald, 'Ali Baba and the Forty Thieves in Arabic from a Bodleian MS', *Journal of the Royal Asiatic Society*, XLII (1910), pp. 327–86.

24   Translated from: 'Die Geschichte von Ali Baba', vol. IV, p. 650.

25   Aboubakr Chraibi, 'Galland's "Ali Baba" and Other Arabic Versions', *Marvels and Tales*, XVIII (2004), pp. 159–69; Muhsin Mahdi, *The Thousand and One Nights* (Leiden, 1995), pp. 72–86.

26   Karl Marx, *Capital: A Critique of Political Economy*, vol. I, trans. Ben Fowkes (Harmondsworth, 1990), p. 493.

27   *Corporis Constitutionum Marchicarum continuatio prima . . . von 1737. bis 1740 . . . colligiret und ans Licht gegeben von Christian Otto Mylius* (Berlin and Halle, 1744), pp. 37–8. Thanks for the information on Prussian house numbering to Bernhard Wittstock (Berlin), who produced the following dissertation based on a five-volume publication on the history of house numbering: Bernhard Wittstock, 'Ziffer Zahl Ordnung. Die Berliner Hausnummer von den Anfängen Ende des 18. Jahrhunderts bis zur Gegenwart im deutschen und europäischen Kontext', inaugural dissertation for the degree of Doktor-Ingenieur (Technische Universität Berlin, 2010).

28   *March-Reglement vor das Herzogthum Schlesien und die Grafschafft Glatz. de Dato Potsdam den 1. Martii 1743* (Bresslau, 1743). Staatsbibliothek zu Berlin, Preussischer Kulturbesitz, call number: 2" Gu 12102. Nr 5.

29  *Königlich Preussisches neu revidiertes March-Reglement vor Seiner Königlichen Majestät sämtliche Provintzien und Lande: De dato Berlin den 5ten Januarii 1752* (Berlin, 1752). Staatsbibliothek zu Berlin, Preussischer Kulturbesitz, call number: 2" Gu 12102. N° 70.

30  Moravský Zemský Archiv, Brno (hereafter MZA), B1 Gubernium, H 193, box 602: Znaimer Kreisamt an mährisches Gubernium, 8 April 1767. Also the Canton-Reglement of 1792 mentions house numbers and orders numbering where it has not yet taken place: Eugen von Frauenholz, *Das Heerwesen in der Zeit des Absolutismus* (Entwicklungsgeschichte des deutschen Heerwesens, 4) (Munich, 1940), pp. 310, 327 (Canton-Reglement, 12 February 1792).

31  MZA, B1, H 193, box 602: Bürgermeister und Rat der Stadt Brno an mährisches Gubernium, 14 March 1767.

32  Jacques-François Guillaute, *Mémoire sur la réformation de la police en France. Soumis au roy en 1749*, ed. Jean Seznec (Paris, 1974).

33  Charles E. Kany, *Life and Manners in Madrid, 1750–1800* (Berkeley, CA, 1932), p. 44.

34  Richard Twiss, *Travels through Portugal and Spain, in 1772 and 1773* (London, 1775), p. 140.

35  Minuta di rapporto, 6 April 1754, quoted in Pietro Montanelli, *Il movimento storico della popolazione di Trieste* (Trieste, 1905), p. 105.

36  Österreichisches Staatsarchiv, Vienna (hereafter ÖStA): Allgemeines Verwaltungsarchiv (hereafter AVA), Hofkanzlei, III A 4 Niederösterreich, box 375, 56 ex May 1753: Instruktion für die niederösterreichische Repräsentation und Kammer, 10 May 1753; IV M 1 Niederösterreich, box 1326, 23 ex March 1754: Hofdekret an niederösterreichische Repräsentation und Kammer, 2 March 1754, f. 30v (insertion: 'without in the process, however, carrying out any further numbering'); cf. Viktor Bibl, *Die Wiener Polizei: Eine kulturhistorische Studie* (Leipzig, Vienna and New York, 1927), pp. 203–5, which does not mention the withdrawal of house numbering.

37  Lars Behrisch, '"Politische Zahlen": Statistik und Rationalisierung der Herrschaft im späten Ancien Régime', *Zeitschrift für historische Forschung*, XXXI (2004), pp. 551–77 (p. 566).

38  Michael Hochedlinger, 'Ein militärischer Bericht über die soziale und wirtschaftliche Lage Tirols im Jahr 1786. Zum Versuch der "militärischen Gleichschaltung" Tirols unter Joseph II (1784–1790)', *Tiroler Heimat*, LXVII (2003), pp. 221–59 (p. 235).

39  AVA, Hofkanzlei, VII A 4 box 2003, 9 ex May 1767: Votum zur Session vom 24 April 1767 and 25 April 1767; the corresponding court decree is only partially available in Vienna. On this cf. Margareth Lanzinger, *Das gesicherte Erbe: Heirat in lokalen und familialen Kontexten, Innichen 1700–1900* (L'Homme Schriften. Reihe zur Feministischen Geschichtswissenschaft, 8) (Vienna, Cologne and Weimar, 2003), pp. 173f.; Hermann Rogger, 'Handwerker und Gewerbetreibende in Innichen seit dem 17. Jahrhundert. Ein Beitrag zur Familien- und allgemeinen Sozialgeschichte dieses Hochpustertaler Marktfleckens', dissertation (University of Innsbruck, 1986), pp. 130, 391; and ÖStA, Kriegsarchiv (hereafter KA), Hofkriegsrat (hereafter HKR) 1769/89/434: Nota Chotek an Hofkriegsrat, 29 July 1769.

40  ÖStA, Haus- Hof- und Staatsarchiv (hereafter HHStA), Kabinettsarchiv: Staatsratsprotokolle (StRP), vol. XXXII (1769/III), No. 2477: Ah. Resolution zu Vortrag der Hofkanzlei vom 30.6.1769, 20 July 1769; this resolution also in KA, HKR 1769/89/398; 1770/74/161 No. 4, as well as AVA, Hofkanzlei, VII A 4 Böhmen, box 1964, 211 ex October 1769, f. 70r–72r.

41  Pronteau, *Numérotages*, pp. 81f.; Alfred Morin, *Le Numérotage des maisons de Troyes (intra-muros), de 1769 à nos Jours* (Troyes, 1983), pp. 10–11.

42  Anton Tantner, *Ordnung der Häuser, Beschreibung der Seelen – Hausnummerierung und Seelenkonskription in der Habsburgermonarchie* (Wiener Schriften zur Geschichte der Neuzeit, 4) (Innsbruck, Vienna and Bozen, 2007).

43  Michael Schattenhofer, 'Bettler, Vaganten und Hausnummern', *Oberbayerisches Archiv*, CIX/1 (1984), pp. 173–5 (p. 173).

44 Friedrich Schütz, 'Rot und Blau – Die Einführung neuer Strassenschilder und Hausnummern 1849–1858 in Mainz', *Mainzer Zeitschrift*, XCIV–XCV (1999–2000), pp. 301–15 (p. 301); K[arl] A[nton] Schaab, *Geschichte der Stadt Mainz* (Mainz, 1844), vol. II, pp. 3, 347, 348.

45 Pronteau, *Numérotages*, pp. 82–6.

46 Franz Häussler, 'Acht Stadtviertel durchnummeriert. Litera-Zahlen galten bis 1938: Strassennamen zweitrangig', *Augsburger Allgemeine Zeitung* (12 September 2000), p. 29; Paul von Stetten, *Beschreibung der Reichs-Stadt Augsburg, nach ihrer Lage jetzigen Verfassung, Handlung und den zu solcher gehörenden Künsten und Gewerben auch ihren anderen Merkwürdigkeiten* (Augsburg, 1788), pp. 8f., 13, 91f.

47 Garrioch, 'House Names', p. 37; Marco Cicchini, 'A New "Inquisition"? Police Reform, Urban Transparency and House Numbering in Eighteenth-century Geneva', *Urban History*, XXXIX (2012), pp. 614–23; Olivier Faron and Alain Pillepich, 'Rue, îlot, quartier: Sur l'identification des espaces citadins à Milan au début du XIXe siécle', *Mélanges de l'École Française de Rome – Italie et Méditerranée*, CV (1993), pp. 333–48 (pp. 338–41).

48 Gusztáv Thirring, *Magyarország Népessége II József korában* [Hungary's Population during the Age of Josef II] (Budapest, 1938), p. 145 (handwritten letter from Joseph II to Ferenc Esterházy, 1 May 1784).

49 [Christian Wilhelm von Dohm], 'Schreiben aus Ungarn', *Deutsches Museum*, vol. I (1785), pp. 58–84 (p. 74) (Order by the royal and imperial governorship in Pressburg/Bratislava, 16 August 1784).

50 Paul von Mitrofanov, *Joseph II: Seine politische und kulturelle Tätigkeit* (Vienna and Leipzig, 1910), vol. I, p. 385. On the opposition by the nobility to recruitment, without going into detail on registration and house numbering: Horst Haselsteiner, *Joseph II und die Komitate Ungarns: Herrscherrecht und ständischer Konstitutionalismus* (Veröffentlichungen des österreichischen Ost- und Südosteuropa-Instituts, 11) (Vienna, Cologne and Graz, 1983).

51  Mitrofanov, *Joseph II*, pp. 382f.; Edith Kotasek, *Feldmarschall Graf Lacy: ein Leben für Österreichs Heer* (Horn, 1956), p. 134.

52  Gustave Thirring, 'Les Recensements de la population en Hongrie sous Joseph II (1784–1787)', *Journal de la Société Hongroise de Statistique*, IX (1931), pp. 201–47 (pp. 207–14).

53  [Dohm], 'Schreiben', pp. 73f (Order by the royal and imperial governorship in Pressburg/Bratislava, 16 August 1784).

54  Thirring, 'Recensements', p. 215.

55  Mitrofanov, *Joseph II*, pp. 386–9.

56  Pierre Ambroise François Choderlos de Laclos, 'Projet de numérotage des rues de Paris', in Choderlos de Laclos, *Oeuvres complètes* (Paris, 1979), pp. 597–600.

57  Pronteau, *Numérotages*, pp. 87–92, 229–31.

58  For example, Basel 1798. Schattenhofer: 'Bettler', p. 174; In the Netherlands, some places were therefore already numbered by 1794, numbering becoming compulsory after 1807. R. Wartena and G. Velthorst, 'Die huisnummering in de gemeente Wisch 1794–1952', *Nederlandsch Archievenblad*, LXXXV (1981), pp. 333–48; Gerard Otten, 'De huisnummering in de huidige gemeente Breda', *Jaarbroek de Oranjeboom*, LXV (2012), pp. 110–67.

59  Carl Ganser, 'Die Wirkungen der französischen Herrschaft, Gesetzgebung und Verwaltung auf das Aachener Wirtschaftsleben', inaugural dissertation (University of Tübingen, 1922), p. 27, http://sylvester.bth.rwth-aachen.de, accessed 4 November 2014; [Wiltrud] Fischer-Pache, 'Hausnumerierung', in *Stadtlexikon Nürnberg (Deutschland)*, http://online-service2.nuernberg.de, accessed 4 November 2014.

60  Benedikt Goebel, '4711. Kurze Geschichte der Hausnummerierung', in *10 + 5 = Gott: Die Macht der Zeichen*, ed. Daniel Tyradellis and Michal S. Friedlander (Cologne, 2004), p. 198; 'Die Nummerierung von 1794', http://history.eau-de-cologne.com, accessed 4 November 2014.

61  [Anonymous], 'Die Bezeichnung der Häuser in Berlin mit Numern', *Berlinische Monatsschrift* (1798), pp. 143–52.

62  Goebel, '4711. Kurze Geschichte', p. 198.

63  Giulio Zorzanello, 'Il centocinquantesimo anniversario della numerazione delle case di Venezia. Note sulla toponomastica veneziana', *Ateneo Veneto*, XXIX (1991), pp. 307–37 (pp. 307–10).

64  On fingerprints see Carlo Ginzburg, *Clues, Myths and the Historical Method* (Baltimore, MD, 2013), pp. 109–11; on Latin American planned towns: Bernhard Siegert, *Passagiere und Papiere: Schreibakte auf der Schwelle zwischen Spanien und Amerika* (Munich, 2006), pp. 142–58.

65  In Münster, for example, houses were numbered in connection with the fire insurance association started in 1768. Mechthild Siekmann, 'Die Brandversicherung im Hochstift Münster 1768–1805: Entstehung, Arbeitsweise, Quellen', *Westfälische Forschungen*, XXXI (1981), pp. 154–68.

66  Ludwig Meyer von Knonau, 'Selbstbiographie Ludwig Meyer's von Knonau in den Jahren 1789–1797', *Zürcher Taschenbuch*, II (1859), pp. 1–71 (pp. 3f.)

67  Národní Archiv, Prag (hereafter NA), České Gubernium (hereafter ČG)-Militare (Mil), 1763–1783, Q 7, box 273: Chrudimer Kreisamt an böhmische Konskriptionskommission, 15 December 1770.

68  Hubert Wank, 'Flüchtige Behausung', in Wilhelm Berger, Klaus Ratschiller and Hubert Wank, *Flucht und Kontrolle. Beiträge zu einer politischen Philosophie der Bewegung* (Reihe Historische Anthropologie, 28) (Berlin, 1996), pp. 95–120 (pp. 107f.)

69  Entry on 'Haus', in Jacob Grimm and Wilhelm Grimm, *Deutsches Wörterbuch* [1877] (Munich, 1991), vol. X: H-Juzen, col. 640–51 (col. 640).

70  MZA, B1, R 93/4B, box 1672: Iglauer Kreisamt an mährisches Gubernium, 1 May 1771.

71  MZA, B1, R 93/4B, box 1672: Mährisches Gubernium an Iglauer Kreisamt, 7 June 1771.

72  Josef Matzke and Josefa Hiller, *Beuren an der Biber. Geschichte eines schwäbischen Dorfes* (Weissenhorn, 1985), pp. 22f., quote 22. Thanks to Manfred Eichhorn for this information.

73  Manfred Eichhorn, *Johann Meyerhofer oder Die Einführung der Hausnummern. Eine Bauernkomödie* (Weinheim, 1994).

74 Cicchini, 'A New "Inquisition"?', p. 620.

75 Walter Benjamin, 'The Paris of the Second Empire in Baudelaire', in *Selected Writings*, vol. IV: *1938–1940*, ed. Howard Eiland and Michael W. Jennings (Cambridge, MA, 2003), pp. 3–92 (p. 26); see also *The Arcades Project*, p. 521.

76 Reuben Rose-Redwood, 'With Numbers in Place: Security, Territory, and the Production of Calculable Space', *Annals of the Association of American Geographers*, CII (2012), pp. 295–319 (p. 311).

77 KA, HKR 1770/74/1026: Protokoll der niederösterreichischen Konskriptionskommission, 12 November 1770.

78 KA, HKR 1770/74/957: Reskript an Neipperg, 28 November 1770.

79 Louis-Sebastien Mercier, *Tableau de Paris*, 2 vols (Paris, 1994), vol. I, Chap. 170, p. 403.

80 Cf. for example KA, HKR 1770/74/861: Nota des Hofkriegsrats an die Hofkanzlei, 5 November 1770.

81 Ibid.

82 Tobias Jakobovits, 'Die Judenabzeichen in Böhmen', *Jahrbuch der Gesellschaft für Geschichte der Juden in der Čechoslovakischen Republik*, III (1931), pp. 145–84 (pp. 170ff.)

83 NA, ČG-Mil 1763–1783, Q 72, box 276: Bunzlauer Kreisamt to böhmisches Gubernium, 20 February 1773

84 NA, ČG-Mil 1763–1783, Q 72, box 276: Böhmisches Gubernium to Bunzlauer Kreisamt, 24 April 1773.

85 NA, ČG-Mil 1763–1783, Q 1, box 270: Kopie eines Reskripts des Hofkriegsrats an das böhmische Generalkommando, 26 May 1773; AVA, Hofkanzlei, IV T 2 Böhmen –1780, box 1526: Hofdekret an mährisches Gubernium, 11 June 1773.

86 KA, Militärhofkommission Nostitz-Rieneck, box 11, Fasz. VII/15: Entwurf, 1792, f. 67r; Adolf Ficker, 'Vorträge über die Vornahme der Volkszählung in Österreich. Gehalten in dem vierten und sechsten Turnus der statistisch administrativen Vorlesungen', *Mittheilungen aus dem Gebiete der Statistik*, XVII (1870), pp. 1–142 (p. 11), Note 2 (Patent 25 October 1804); see also the autobiography of Ignaz Briess: Ignaz Briess, *Schilderungen aus*

*dem Prerauer Ghettoleben vom Jahre 1838–1848: mit Streiflichtern bis an die Gegenwart und Jugenderinnerungen eines 78jährigen* (Brno, 1912), p. 9, l.

87 Wienerisches Diarium, oder Nachrichten von Staats, vermischten, und gelehrten Neuigkeiten, 5 January 1771, No. 2.

88 Wienerisches Diarium, oder Nachrichten von Staats, vermischten, und gelehrten Neuigkeiten, 2 February 1771, No. 10.

89 Wilhelm A. Bauer and Otto Erich Deutsch, *Mozart: Briefe und Aufzeichnungen. Gesamtausgabe*, 7 vols (Kassel, 1963–1975), vol. III, pp. 95, 112, 154, 225, 251f., 269f., 300f., 370; vol. IV, pp. 44, 66, 133; vol. VI, p. 364.

90 MZA, B1, R 93/16A, box 1679: Barbara Schönhoferin to mährisch-schlesisches Gubernium, 1 May 1784; Mährisch-Schlesisches Gubernium to Olmützer Kreisamt, 6 May 1784; Obristlieutenant v Rechtenbach to Olmützer Kreisamt, 17 June 1784; Olmützer Kreisamt to mährisch-schlesisches Gubernium, 24 June 1784; Aktennotiz, 1 July 1784.

91 The relevant procedure in Archiv Města Brna, Brno (hereafter AMB), Stará spisovna: In publicis (SS in pub) 1784–1789 (1851), Inv. No. 2774, 776/51 box 326.

92 AMB, SS in pub 1784–1789 (1851), Inv. No. 2774, 776/51 box 326: Aktennotiz, 11 April 1818.

93 AMB, SS in pub 1784–1789 (1851), Inv. No. 2774, 776/51 box 326: Bericht of the Brünner Magistrat to the Brünner Kreisamt, 27 June 1818.

94 Ibid.

95 A concordance list is given in Anton Behsel, *Verzeichniss aller in der kaiserl. königl. Haupt- und Residenzstadt Wien mit ihren Vorstädten befindlichen Häuser, mit genauer Angabe der älteren, mittleren und neuesten Nummerirungen, der dermahligen Eigenthümer und Schilder, der Strassen und Plätze, der Grund-Obrigkeiten, dann der Polizey- und Pfarr-Bezirke* (Vienna, 1829).

96 Ficker, 'Vorträge', p. 21.

97 Hertha Wohlrab and Felix Czeike, 'Die Wiener Häusernummern und Strassentafeln', *Wiener Geschichtsblätter*,

XXVII (1972), pp. 333–52 (pp. 343–50); 'Häusernumerierung', in Felix Czeike, ed., *Historisches Lexikon Wien in fünf Bänden* (Vienna, 1992–7), vol. III, pp. 89f.; 'Grundbuchs-Einlagezahl', in Czeike, *Historisches Lexikon*, vol. II, p. 622.

98  Beschluss des Wiener Gemeinderats über die einheitliche Numerierung der Gebäude, 24 October 1958, at www.wien.gv.at, accessed 4 November 2014.

99  Information kindly supplied by Martina Grečenková, Stephan Templ and Gerald Schubert.

100  [Johann Erich Biester], 'Die Bezeichnung der Häuser in Berlin mit Numern', *Berlinische Monatsschrift* (1798), pp. 143–52 (p. 148).

101  Mark Twain, 'The Chicago of Europe', *Chicago Daily Tribune* (3 April 1892), www.twainquotes.com, accessed 4 November 2014, also in Twain, *The Complete Essays of Mark Twain*, ed. Charles Neider (Garden City, NJ, 1963), pp. 87–98 (pp. 89, 93f.)

102  Charles Merruau, *Rapport sur la nomenclature des rues et le numérotage des maisons de Paris* (Paris, n.d. [*c.* 1860]), p. 48.

103  John Pinkerton, *Recollections of Paris, in the Years 1802–3–4–5*, 2 vols (London, 1806), vol. I, p. 47.

104  Reuben S. Rose-Redwood, 'Indexing the Great Ledger of the Community: Urban House Numbering, City Directories, and the Production of Spatial Legibility', *Journal of Historical Geography*, XXXIV (2008), pp. 286–310 (p. 292); Clement Biddle, *The Philadelphia Directory* (Philadelphia, PA, 1791), http://archive.org, accessed 4 November 2014.

105  Reuben S. Rose-Redwood, '"A Regular State of Beautiful Confusion": Governing by Numbers and the Contradictions of Calculable Space in New York City', *Urban History*, XXXIX (2012–14), pp. 624–38 (pp. 627f.)

106  Pronteau, *Numérotages*, pp. 99–133; see also Benjamin, *The Arcades Project*, p. 521.

107  Heinrich Adami, 'Wien. Wochen-Courier der Theaterzeitung', *Allgemeine Theaterzeitung* (21 August 1847), No. 200, pp. 798f.

108  Michael Winkler, *Winkler's Orientirungs-Plan der k.k. Reichshaupt- und Residenzstadt Wien mit ihren acht umliegenden Vorstadt-Bezirken* (Vienna, 1863), Foreword (unpaginated).

109 Wohlrab and Czeike, 'Häusernummern', pp. 343–50; Felix Czeike, ed., 'Häusernumerierung', in *Historisches Lexikon*, vol. III, pp. 89f.

110 'Verordnung betreffend polizeiliche Nummerirung der Häuser', 11 February 1865, in *Amtliche Sammlung der seit Annahme der Gemeindeordnung vom Jahr 1859 erlassenen Verordnungen und wichtigeren Gemeindebeschlüsse der Stadt Zürich* (Zurich, 1869), vol. III, pp. 40–42.

111 Wittstock, 'Ziffer', pp. 123, 154–60.

112 See also the following lists of methods: Merruau, *Rapport sur la nomenclature des rues et le numérotage des maisons de Paris*, pp. 47–51; Catherine Farvacque-Vitkovic et al., *Street Addressing and the Management of Cities* (Washington, DC, 2005), pp. 146–62, http://hdl.handle.net/10986/7342, accessed 4 November 2014; Wittstock, 'Ziffer', pp. 84–148; with instructive graphics: 'House Numbering', at http://en.wikipedia.org, accessed 4 November 2014.

113 Fischer-Pache, 'Hausnumerierung'.

114 As an aid to location in the period before Google Maps the following was useful: Jonathan Del Mar, *Indicatore Anagrafico di Venezia* (Venice, 1996).

115 Kany, *Life*, p. 44.

116 Wittstock, 'Ziffer', p. 119.

117 Rose-Redwood, 'Indexing', p. 300.

118 Pronteau, *Numérotages*, pp. 54, 122, 231; Farvacque-Vitkovic et al., *Street Addressing*, p. 148; email from Françoise Guiguet, 20 April 2013.

119 Pronteau, *Numérotages*, p. 53; Farvacque-Vitkovic et al., *Street Addressing*, pp. 12, 17, 54–101.

120 Ivo Andrić, *The Bridge on the Drina*, trans. Lovett F. Edwards (Belgrade, 2011), pp. 233–5.

121 Joseph Roth, *The Radetzky March*, trans. Michael Hoffmann (London, 2003), p. 143.

122 On observations about the Habsburg Monarchy from the perspective of postcolonial studies, see Ursula Prutsch, 'Habsburg Postcolonial', in *Habsburg postcolonial:*

*Machtstrukturen und kollektives Gedächtnis*, ed. Johannes Feichtinger, Ursula Prutsch and Moritz Csáky (Innsbruck, 2003), pp. 33–43 (p. 36; also p. 43, n. 17 on house numbering).

123 Report submitted by M. Lucien Lambeau, in the name of the 1re Sous-commission, on a paper on the numbering of houses, in *Commission municipale du Vieux Paris. Année 1900. Procès-Verbaux* (Paris, 1901), pp. 72–8.

124 Birgit Wolf, *Sprache in der DDR: Ein Wörterbuch* (Berlin and New York, 2000), p. 87.

125 'Goldene Hausnummern', *Märkische Oderzeitung* (10 November 2008), at www.moz.de.

126 *KommA21 Bayern aktuell. InfoNetzwerk für nachhaltige Kommunalentwicklung*, 2 June 2004, pp. 49f, at www.bestellen.bayern.de.

127 Eckhardt Kauntz, 'Grüne Hausnummer als Auszeichnung', *Frankfurter Allgemeine Zeitung* (29 June 1996), p. 4; '"Grüne Hausnummer" für 100 Öko-Punkte', *Süddeutsche Zeitung* (29 June 1996), p. 5; Andreas Blum, Clemens Deilmann and Frank-Stefan Neubauer, 'Eco-labelling for Buildings', in *Towards Sustainable Building*, ed. Nicola Maiellaro (Dordrecht, Boston, MA, and London, 2001), pp. 43–58 (p. 47).

128 Roland Keth, 'Gütesiegel oder Stigmatisierung? Skepsis im Stadtrat zu grüner Hausnummer', *Wormser Zeitung* (21 October 2005), available at www.genios.de, accessed 4 November 2014.

129 Tyradellis and Friedlander, ed., *10 + 5*, pp. 94, 199.

130 Laurie Becklund, 'Reagans Easing Into Private Life as Californians', *Los Angeles Times* (19 November 1988), available at http://articles.latimes.com.

131 'Hausnummer verändern?', www.esoterikforum.at, accessed 4 November 2014.

132 *Widerst@nd! – MUND* (Medienunabhängiger Nachrichtendienst), Saturday, 11 March 2000 (newsletter sent by email, first mention of a house number in an appointments diary not archived on the Web).

133 At https://web.archive.org/web/20020204001859/http://radiowiderhall.cjb.net/, accessed 4 November 2014; latest radio

programmes: http://o94.at/radio/sendereihe/ radio_widerhall, accessed 4 November 2014.

134 At http://blackbox.net/c/Anarchy/Botschaft_besorgter_ BuergerInnen/info/index.htm, accessed 22 November 2006, (inactive as of 2014).

135 Roland Barthes, *Empire of Signs*, trans. Richard Howard (New York, 1983), pp. 33–7; Farvacque-Vitkovic et al., *Street Addressing*, p. 9.

136 Farvacque-Vitkovic et al., *Street Addressing*, pp. 36, 38, 48.

137 Kristina Läsker, 'Auf dem Weg nach Irgendwo', *Süddeutsche Zeitung* (5 January 2005), p. 12.

138 Email from Michael Maiwald, 22 November 2006.

139 City GIS for the Emirate of Ras al-Khaimah, www2.geog.uni-heidelberg.de, accessed 4 November 2014.

140 Andreas Becker, 'Stadt ohne Strassennamen. Lost in Seoul', *Frankfurter Rundschau*, 17 May 2006, available at www.genios.de, accessed 4 November 2014; Hoo Nam Seelmann, 'Abschied vom kolonialen Adresssystem', *Neue Zürcher Zeitung* (30 August 2013); 'Addresses in South Korea', http://en.wikipedia.org, accessed 4 November 2014.

141 This procedure described from the point of view of a Google member of staff: Ian J. Goodfellow et al., 'Multi-digit Number Recognition from Street View Imagery using Deep Convolutional Neural Networks', available online using citation arXiv:1312.6082v4 [cs.CV].

## Further Reading

Farvacque-Vitkovic, Catherine, et al., *Street Addressing and the Management of Cities* (Washington, DC, 2005)

Gallery of House Numbers
  Website set up in 2002 by Anton Tantner, displaying more than 100 photos of historic house numbers.
  http://housenumbers.tantner.net

Pronteau, Jeanne, *Les Numérotages des maisons de Paris du XVe siècle à nos jours* (Publications de la sous-commission de recherches d'histoire municipale contemporaine VIII) (Paris, 1966)

Rose-Redwood, Reuben, and Anton Tantner, ed., 'History of Urban House Numbering', special section of *Urban History*, XXXIX (2012–14), pp. 607–79

Containing:

Cicchini, Marco, 'A New "Inquisition"? Police Reform, Urban Transparency and House Numbering in Eighteenth-century Geneva', pp. 614–23

Harris, Richard, and Robert Lewis: 'Numbers Didn't Count: The Streets of Colonial Bombay and Calcutta', pp. 639–58

Rose-Redwood, Reuben S., '"A Regular State of Beautiful Confusion": Governing by Numbers and the Contradictions of Calculable Space in New York City', pp. 624–38

—, and Anton Tantner, 'Introduction: Governmentality, House Numbering and the Spatial History of the Modern City', pp. 607–13

Vuolteenaho, Jani, 'Numbering the Streetscape: Mapping the Spatial History of Numerical Street Names in Europe', pp. 659–79

Tantner, Anton, *Ordnung der Häuser, Beschreibung der Seelen – Hausnummerierung und Seelenkonskription in der Habsburgermonarchie* (Wiener Schriften zur Geschichte der Neuzeit 4) (Innsbruck, Vienna and Bozen, 2007)

Wittstock, Bernhard, 'Ziffer Zahl Ordnung. Die Berliner Hausnummer von den Anfängen Ende des 18. Jahrhunderts bis zur Gegenwart im deutschen und europäischen Kontext'. Inaugural Dissertation for the degree of Doktor-Ingenieur (Technische Universität Berlin, 2010). (Based on Bernhard Wittstock, *Die Berliner Hausnummer. Von den Anfängen Ende des 18. Jahrhunderts bis zur Gegenwart im deutschen und europäischen Kontext*, 5 vols (Berlin, 2008))

## Photo Acknowledgements

The author and publishers wish to express their thanks to the below sources of illustrative material and/or permission to reproduce it:

Photos author: pp. 22, 39, 44, 46, 47, 48, 49, 50, 56, 67, 68, 69, 70, 71, 80, 81, 85, 87, 91, 92, 97, 100, 101, 102, 107, 109, 113, 114, 115, 118, 119, 120, 128, 129, 130, 139, 143, 149, 150, 152, 155, 156, 157, 158, 159, 163, 168, 169, 170, 172, 173, 174, 175, 176, 177, 179, 182, 183; photo Dinkum: p. 135; photo Eye Ubiquitous/Rex Features: p. 7; photo © Philip Gould/CORBIS: pp. 180–81; photo Image Broker/Rex Features: p. 127; photo © Bob Krist/CORBIS: pp. 140–41; photos mattes: pp. 66, 88, 124; photo © Nicholls: Alistair/Arcaid/CORBIS: p. 162; photo Olybrius: p. 134; photo Avital Pinnick, 2010: pp. 110–11; photo © Richard Powers/Arcaid/CORBIS: p. 178; photo © Heini Schneebeli/Edifice/CORBIS: p. 123; photo Douglas Scott/Alamy: pp. 166–7; photo Sonia Sevilla: p. 86; photo User:Sir kiss: p. 142.

brian, the copyright holder of the image on p. 12, Jean-François Gornet, the copyright holder of the images on pp. 79, 90, 99, 131, 138, 144, 148, 151, 164, and Thaddeus Quintin, the copyright holder of the image on p. 137, have published them online under conditions imposed by a Creative Commons Attribution-Share Alike 2.0 Generic license; mattes, the copyright holder of the image on p. 14, has published it online under conditions imposed by a Creative Commons Attribution 2.0 Germany license; Jøra, the copyright holder of the image on p. 57, has published it online under conditions imposed by a Creative Commons Attribution 3.0 Unported license; Oxfordian Kissuth, the copyright holder of the image on p. 72, Joergens.mi, the copyright holder of the image on p. 73, Josef Moser, the copyright holder of the image on p. 74, 4028mdk09, the copyright holder of the images on pp. 75, 93, 94, 103, 104–5, 112, Calenugkan, the copyright holder of the image on p. 76, Wolfgang Sauber, the copyright holder of the images on pp. 77, 126, Coyau, the copyright holder of the images on pp. 78,